# The Killing of Chief Crazy Horse

three eyewitness views by
the Indian, Chief He Dog
the Indian-white, William Garnett
the White doctor, Valentine McGillycuddy

*with commentary by*
**Carroll Friswold**

*edited, with introduction, by*
**Robert A. Clark**

University of Nebraska Press
Lincoln and London

Copyright © 1976 by The Arthur H. Clark Company
Preface to the Bison Book Edition copyright © 1988 by the
University of Nebraska Press
All rights reserved
Manufactured in the United States of America

First Bison Book printing: 1988
Most recent printing indicated by the first digit below:
                              7    8    9    10

Library of Congress Cataloging-in-Publication Data
The Killing of Chief Crazy Horse.
  Reprint. Originally published: Glendale, Calif.: A. H. Clark Co., 1976.
(Hidden springs of Custeriana; 4)
  Bibliography: p.
  Includes index.
  1. Crazy Horse, ca. 1842–1877. 2. Oglala Indians—Biography. 3.
Indians of North America—Wars—1866–1895. I. He Dog, 1837–
1936. II. Garnett, William, 1855–1929. III. McGillycuddy, Valentine,
1849–1939. IV. Friswold, Carroll. V. Clark, Robert A., 1948– .
E99.03K54 1988    973.8'3'0924 [B]    87-30209
ISBN 0-8032-1442-1
ISBN 0-8032-6330-9 (pbk.)

Reprinted by arrangement with The Arthur H. Clark Company

∞

# Contents

# Illustrations

# Preface to the Bison Book Edition

The publication of documentary historical materials significantly widens public access to first-hand evidence surrounding important historical incidents, and in addition removes the filter that interpreters of history may slip in place to refine the image to fit their biases.

For three generations the Arthur H. Clark Company has sought to publish documentary histories dealing with American history, of which this work is but a small part. For a variety of reasons, these publications have been issued in small editions–only three hundred copies were printed of *The Killing of Crazy Horse*. It was sold out within a year of publication. We are pleased that the University of Nebraska Press has chosen to make the work available to a larger audience.

As noted in the original preface, we found it necessary, in preparing the manuscript for press, to expand on the late Mr. Friswold's commentary by adding an historical introduction, a reading list, and an index. We chose not to dispute or alter his comments. We remain unconvinced, however, regarding his support of the authenticity of the photograph of Crazy Horse. In view of the Oglala's short time at Red Cloud Agency, and his alleged aversion to the white man's shadow catcher, it is unlikely that such a photograph exists. Analyses of this and other photographs purported to be Crazy Horse have been made and substantial proof is lacking.

## The Killing of Chief Crazy Horse

In reviewing materials not seen prior to the original preparation of the historical introduction, I have not changed my assessment of the sequence of events that occurred in Nebraska in 1877. I have become more convinced of the duplicity of interpreter Frank Grouard. The conflicts and jealousies among the agency chiefs seem to me even more likely to have been the principal cause of rumors about Crazy Horse's rebelliousness, resulting in his arrest and death. These men of the plains had been robbed of their power and freedom, and sought by insidious methods to destroy new rivals who challenged the little power they clung to at Red Cloud and Spotted Tail agencies. The Hinman interviews and Ricker tablets provide additional support to the contention that the soldier's bayonet killed Crazy Horse, not the knife of Little Big Man or the deflected knife of the victim.

What follows is the sad tale of a brave and proud man's death, a death that symbolized the unworthy end of a unique culture. May the dignity of all men be held in greater value.

R.A.C.

# Acknowledgments

Every student of American frontier history owes a bow and a salute to my good friend from Chicago, Fred Hackett, for the recognition and preservation of much of the material used in this study. Mr. Hackett was one of the founders of the Chicago Corral of the Westerners, he used to travel with the Buffalo Bill Wild West Show, and every year since about 1905 he visits the Pine Ridge Indian Reservation in South Dakota. In that length of time he had come to know nearly all the prominent Indians of that region, especially the older ones, many of whom were veterans of the Indian Wars and the Custer Battle. So much was he appreciated that he was made a member of the Oglala Tribal Council and bore the Indian name of "Wazeepa" — Pine on the Hill. From time to time Fred would be offered and would acquire something special, such as a battle relic, beadwork, dresses, weapons, and on a few occasions written material. On one such occasion he acquired the correspondence and records left on the death of the famous guide and interpreter William Garnett — these included Garnett's manuscript of the killing of Crazy Horse and the letters of Dr. McGillycuddy, plus much other material. Many of these items have been held in the Hackett Collection for over thirty years and would be impossible to duplicate. Chief He Dog's narrative is also from Mr. Hackett's collection.

Also, my sincere thanks to the Stackpole Company for permission to quote regarding Little Bat from their *Fighting Indian Warriors* by Brininstool, 1953. The late

### The Killing of Chief Crazy Horse

Mari Sandoz was kind enough to grant permission to quote from her writing in the *Brand Book* of the New York Posse of Westerners. Through the courtesy of the Nebraska State Historical Society I am able to include the pictures of Little Bat's family, He Dog, Little Big Man, Woman's Dress and Touch the Cloud. The other pictures are from my own collection.

CARROLL FRISWOLD

# Preface

In the annals of the Sioux, an old Oglala winter count beginning in 1759 has the following notation to correspond with the Christian calendar year of 1877, *Tasunka witko ktepi*–Crazy Horse was killed.

Those three words, *Tasunka witko ktepi,* describe the event which we will examine herein, some hundred years after it occurred, through the accounts of participants, eyewitnesses and officials.

It has all the elements of a classical tragedy–the envy, greed and jealousy of the rival chiefs; the treachery of the victim's former friend, Frank Grouard; the plotting and scheming of Lieutenant William P. Clark; the stubbornness of General Crook. And the final scene, the violent death of the warrior, is as stark and inevitable as though it were from a play by one of the Greek masters of two thousand years ago.

The accounts might almost be called three-dimensional, as we are going to look at the event from three widely different angles. First we will view the incident from the viewpoint of an Indian sympathetic to the victim, Chief He Dog, the boyhood friend and lifelong companion of Crazy Horse; next, the account of William Garnett, who had both red and white parentage and who was on the inside of all the happenings as the guide and interpreter for Lieutenant William P. Clark, Second Cavalry staff officer and personal representative to General Crook; and lastly the remembrances of the famous Dr. Valentine McGillycuddy, medical officer on duty that late summer afternoon at Camp Robinson in Nebraska, who attended Crazy Horse from the time he was bayonetted until he died just before midnight on September 5, 1877. His correspondence with Garnett on this and related topics rounds out the primary source accounts.

In addition to these three accounts of the incident, the late Mr. Friswold provided the publishers with supplementary materials both textual and illustrative. The manuscript materials were being held at the time of Mr. Friswold's death in 1969, and when the project was finally brought into production in 1976, we decided to use all the materials left with us, including Mr. Friswold's comments introducing each item. All of the text in the volume is his with the exception of the introduction, bibliography, and index, which were prepared by the editor.

The text of the documents is unaltered from the transcription provided by Mr. Friswold. It was his intent to retain the individual style of each document. In preparing the materials, the editor found need to refer to other sources for background events, to identify certain characters, and to explore the conflicting points in the accounts. The modest introduction that follows is the result, and any errors therein are solely our responsibility.

Robert A. Clark

# Introduction

Eight years prior to Custer's famed march toward the Little Big Horn, leaders of the Sioux nation met with government commissioners at Fort Laramie in Dakota Territory to sign an agreement concerning lands upon which the associated bands in the nation then lived. Chiefs of the Brulé, Oglala, Miniconjous and Yanktonais bands of the Sioux, and of the northern Arapaho, signed a treaty on April 29, 1868, establishing all of the present state of South Dakota west of the Missouri River as Indian Reservation land. In addition, the right to hunt on lands above the North Platte and on the Republican rivers was provided for, as long as justified by the number of buffalo.

Red Cloud, a leading chief of the Oglala Sioux, refused to attend this conference and signing. He preferred the use of force to meet the white man's encroachments. The army was at this time attempting to maintain and protect the Bozeman Trail to mines in what is now southern Montana. The road ran directly through the south side of the Yellowstone River watershed, favorite hunting ground for the Sioux and northern Cheyenne. Red Cloud fought and won a war with the army on this ground during the winter and summer of 1866-67. He watched with pride as the army abandoned the forts throughout the spring and summer of 1868. By fall, satisfied that his victory was complete, he rode into Fort Laramie to sign the treaty. In return for promising to give up the ways of war, the Big Horn-Powder River country south of the Yellowstone was

15

given to the Indians as unceded territory, forbidden to whites, for the use of the Sioux, Cheyenne, and Arapaho tribes.

Red Cloud settled down under government supervision, honored by the whites and exerting great influence among the Sioux at his agency. There were, however, bands of Sioux and Cheyenne still in the unceded territory who had refused to have anything to do with the treaty. They remained in the north, living as their fathers had and protecting the hunting grounds from the encroachments by outsiders, red and white. Here the leadership of chiefs such as Two Moon, Sitting Bull, and Crazy Horse was nurtured, in a land where life was free and unrestrained by white civilization, traditional in nature, and very different from that of the settled bands at the agencies.[1]

With the turning of a new decade, Americans in the settled eastern states and burgeoning Far West looked forward to the nation's Centennial with optimism. Like a vine sending tendrils over freshly cleared soil, the railroads were expanding across the continent. The summer of '73 saw a small band of surveyors (with a cavalry escort commanded by George Custer) move up the north bank of the Yellowstone River, plotting a route for a northern transcontinental line. The project was halted by the financial panic of 1873.

Movement of the whites into this vast northwest land could not be halted so easily, though. The following

---

[1] There have been numerous published works dealing with the history of the northern Plains Indians to which the reader is referred for detailed treatment of the above brief sketch. Among them are the works of George E. Hyde and James C. Olson, cited in the bibliography of this work. These titles, among others, contain numerous references in their notes and bibliographies to primary and secondary treatment of these and associated matters.

summer brought new irritation to the Indians when an expedition was sent to examine the country "in and about the Northern Fork of the Sheyenne, shown on the maps as the Belle Fourche: also the country south of it in the vicinity of Bear Butte, especially South and West of Bear Butte. . ." Once again it was Custer who led his force out from Fort Lincoln, this time southward across the heart of the reservation and into a sacred place of the Sioux – the Black Hills. Custer's column was well armed in case it should encounter opposition, but it proved unnecessary. The Indians seemed passively resigned to what was happening and offered no resistance. The return of the expedition brought glistening reports of gold, both enthusiastic and well publicized. With the coming of winter 1874, a few miners had reached the hills. By the following summer the rush was on. The government was hard pressed to justify this blatant violation of the 1868 treaty.[2]

It seemed that the best chance the government had of preventing an ugly incident between the Sioux and the prospectors was to obtain permission from the Indians for mining in the hills. In September 1875 the Allison Commission went to the Red Cloud Agency in north-western Nebraska. They first made unsuccessful offers for purchase or lease of the hills. An attempt was then made to at least obtain mineral rights to the ore. A refusal to cooperate in each instance was all the Commission received. The disgruntled commissioners returned

---

[2] A recent work dealing specifically with Custer's march to the Black Hills is Herbert Krause and Gary D. Olson, *Prelude to Glory, a Newspaper Accounting of Custer's 1874 Expedition to the Black Hills,* (Sioux Falls, S.D., 1974). Another fine work on this topic is Donald Jackson, *Custer's Gold: The United States Cavalry Expedition of 1874,* (New Haven, Conn., 1966).

to Washington and filed a report which recommended the acquisition of the land over any objection the Indians might make.

Washington found itself with a very flammable situation on its hands. In November 1875 all non-agency Indians were ordered to report to the agencies by January 31, 1876, or provoke the wrath of the army. The absurdity of demanding large camps to march hundreds of miles in mid-winter in order to relinquish their own hunting rights was seemingly unapparent to the government. The response of the hunting bands in the north was negligible, and a campaign against the "hostiles" was begun in the spring of 1876.

A strategy designed to trap the roving bands on their hunting grounds was devised. Three columns were sent into the Big Horn-Powder River country: Brigadier General Alfred Terry's, entering from the east; Brigadier General George Crook's from the south; and Colonel John Gibbon's from the west. Their object was to converge somewhere near the confluence of the Big Horn and Yellowstone rivers, force the surrender of any Indians in that territory, and transport them to the agencies.[3]

The failure of this campaign to achieve its goals is well known. Major battles occurred on June 17 and 25, involving General Crook, and Custer's Seventh Cavalry from Terry's column, respectively. Crook was forced to turn back from the Rosebud River and head south to recoup his losses. Custer stepped into a hornet's nest on the Little Big Horn, resulting in one of the most success-

---

[3] The campaign of 1876, and particularly the Battle of the Little Big Horn, have been more than thoroughly covered in the last hundred years in innumerable books and articles. An excellent survey of the campaign can be found in Edgar I. Stewart, *Custer's Luck,* (Norman, 1955).

ful Indian victories of the nineteenth century, and its most publicized frontier battle. In both of these battles, the name of Crazy Horse of the Oglalas achieved a renown among red and white men as one of the finest military leaders in the Sioux nation.

Word of the defeat of the Seventh Cavalry and the death of almost 250 men reached the States during the celebration of the nation's Centennial, and the shock effect was widespread. A great cry for revenge rose up and soon a number of revisions in Indian affairs were made. On July 22 the military assumed control of all agencies and the Sioux Reservation, replacing the various civil and religious appointees who had been in control since the end of the Civil War. The inhabitants were to be treated as prisoners of war. On August 15, Congress took the unceded Powder River country and the Black Hills from the Sioux for alleged violation of the treaty of 1868. They were accused of making war on the United States. In September a new commission was sent to the Spotted Tail and Red Cloud Agencies with an agreement composed of these conditions: [4]

1. Relinquishment of the Black Hills
2. Receipt of all rations at the Missouri River
3. Permission for three roads to be built across the Reservation to the Black Hills

The commissioners obtained the chiefs' signatures at those two agencies only by threatening to cut off all rations. They avoided the stipulation contained in the treaty of 1868 requiring the signature of three-fourths of the male members of the tribe on any treaty concerning land cessions by calling the document an "Agreement." The commissioners then proceeded to the agen-

---

[4] Schmitt, *Autobiography of George Crook,* 217; see also Robinson, *History of the Sioux Indians,* 440-42.

cies on the Missouri and by using similar coercion gained the signatures of the chiefs at those locations. Troop strength at the agencies was boosted and a great many arms and horses were confiscated, especially at Red Cloud's agency, where that proud chief was as usual making life miserable for his agent.[5]

The Big Horn and Yellowstone Expedition's forces did their best to track down and punish the Sioux after the battle on the Little Big Horn, but stirred up more dust than hostiles. Finally Crook's advance column stumbled on the camp of American Horse at Slim Buttes, September 9, 1876. A few braves were killed, a few others captured, and the rest chased off. It was a lonely victory for the frontier army in what had turned out to be a long summer.

As the fighting season of the Plains Indians waned, a wish for peace entered the hearts of many. Crazy Horse and others, however, refused to listen to these wishes. Crook and Colonel Nelson A. Miles were still in pursuit, commanding the newly organized Powder River Expedition. Crook's cavalry, under Colonel Ranald Mackenzie, surprised the Cheyenne camp of Dull Knife and Little Wolf in the mountains on November 6, and roundly defeated it. The survivors slipped away, through severe weather, and joined the camp of Crazy Horse. The Sioux took the Cheyennes into camp and shared their supplies. The camp in the Wolf Mountains now contained roughly three thousand people, and to maintain a food supply in mid-winter taxed the hunters to the extreme.[6]

---

[5] Hyde, *Red Cloud's Folk*, 284-85.

[6] Though Hyde states in *Spotted Tail's Folk*, 238-39, that Crazy Horse turned away these Cheyennes, thus gaining their hatred, the government records he utilized for *Red Cloud's Folk* showed few Cheyenne coming in to the agencies that winter, p. 287. The size of

A combination of circumstances was forcing the last of the wild Sioux to take actions that the entire summer campaign of the army had been unable to do. When the fist of anger fell on the agencies in late summer 1876, many of the Indians residing there had fled into the old hunting grounds. The great slaughter of buffalo by the whites for hides was in full swing, and the natural food resources of the land were declining dramatically. Suffering and hardship began to take their toll. The recalcitrant bands decided in council to send emissaries to Colonel Miles at Fort Keogh on the Tongue River. In mid-December a Sioux delegation neared the fort, five chiefs leading them as they approached on horseback. Before the army staff had time to react, a band of Miles' Crow scouts, the Sioux's bitter enemies, rushed out and killed the five. The rest of the delegation raced back to the mountains, all hope of peace devastated.[7]

Colonel Miles went after them with determination in late December. On January 1, 1877, he began a running battle with the large camp in the mountains. By the eighth, lack of supplies and forage had forced Miles to return to the fort, but the damage was done. The Indians retreated into the upper Big Horn country with their wounds smarting, and by late January the camp was forced to splinter due to the strain of feeding so many off limited resources.

Crook had given up pursuit in late fall and was busy sending out peace-talkers by December. His first offers

the camp, as estimated in Anderson, "Indian Peace Talkers," 239, indicates a strain on the resources of the surrounding lands, and for this reason some of the refugees may have been turned away. The presence of Cheyenne in the Crazy Horse camp is noted also in Olson, *Red Cloud and the Sioux Problem,* 226-27.

[7] Anderson, "Peace Talkers," 236; Hyde, *Red Cloud's Folk,* 289.

were simply unconditional surrender. There was little response. But the battles in the Wolf Mountains cost the war faction prestige among the Indians, and those who championed peace gained influence. Major Julius W. Mason, Third Cavalry, received word of peace-feelers at his headquarters at Camp Robinson, and telegraphed Crook for permission to begin negotiations.[8] Spotted Tail, uncle of Crazy Horse[9] and much respected Brulé chief at his own agency, was approached on recommendation of Crook. But Spotted Tail refused to carry unconditional terms to the Sioux who were off the reservation. Consequently George Sword[10] of the Red Cloud Agency led thirty persons out in search of the hostiles on January 16, 1877. He experienced limited success by persuading a small group of Cheyennes to come in, which they did in March, but in the meantime bigger plans were in the making.

Early in February, Crook came to Camp Robinson and received word of the battles in the Wolf Mountains. He set out for Camp Sheridan and the Spotted Tail Agency, forty-three miles to the east on Beaver Creek, a southerly tributary to the White River. He felt it was imperative to induce Spotted Tail to aid in bringing in the hostiles. Runners were coming in with reports of strong desires for peace among many of those in the mountains. Spotted Tail was able to obtain good terms from Crook. The general promised to do his best

---

[8] For an excellent review of the peace overtures to the hostiles in the winter of 1876-77, see Anderson, "Indian Peace-Talkers," pp. 233-54. Mason's involvement in the negotiations appear on pp. 239-40.

[9] Two of Spotted Tail's sisters were married to Crazy Horse's father, also named Crazy Horse. Hyde, *Spotted Tail's Folk,* 13.

[10] Sword's Indian name was Hunts the Enemy. Olson, *Red Cloud,* 237.

to secure an agency for the Sioux in the Powder River country, although he still required surrender of all arms and ponies. Also mentioned was the good possibility of a buffalo hunt in the fall. Spotted Tail set out with two hundred picked men on February 13, carrying these terms.[11] The fact that army headquarters was almost totally ignorant of the conditions surrounding the peace overtures is vividly shown in Sherman's remark that Spotted Tail went in search of Crazy Horse on his own initiative.[12]

The competition between Miles and Crook to gain credit for the surrender of the Indians was intense. Miles had sent out Johnny Brughier and Sweet Taste Woman on February 1. According to statements later made by Cheyennes who had been in the mountains at this time, the two emissaries carried a similar promise of a northern agency, this time from Miles, and they arrived with this proposal prior to Spotted Tail's delegation.[13] According to the Cheyenne statements, the Indians began moving toward Fort Keogh, but they were intercepted in late February by runners from Spotted Tail. Several councils were held at the different camps, and most of the bands decided to turn themselves in at either the Red Cloud or Spotted Tail agencies. Brughier later reported that the hostiles were bribed away from Miles with liberal terms, but one of

---

[11] Crook's promise of an agency in the northern country is mentioned in Anderson, "Peace Talkers," 244; Schmitt, *Autobiography of General Crook*, 215; Sandoz, *Crazy Horse*, 348. Bourke disputes this in *On the Border with Crook*, 396 ff. However, Bourke erred in stating that Spotted Tail returned to the agency from his mission early in January, when records show that he did not leave until February 13. The promise of a buffalo hunt is mentioned in Jesse Lee's account found in Brininstool, *Crazy Horse*, 15.

[12] Anderson, "Peace Talkers," 244.           [13] *Ibid.,* 246.

the major factors in enticing them south was no doubt the prestige of Spotted Tail. Miles' disappointment was hardly softened when a small band of three hundred under Two Moon and Hump continued north to Fort Keogh and surrendered to him on April 22.

Spotted Tail returned to Camp Sheridan on April 5, and reported success. The various camps were creeping towards the agencies, hampered by poor grazing and lack of supplies. Red Cloud was asked to take a supply train to meet the camps and facilitate their surrender. He had been stripped of authority at his agency because of rebelliousness, and it was rumored that considerable rewards of status and property were offered in return for his aid.[14] He soon set out with supplies.

On April 14, the first of the camps arrived at the Spotted Tail Agency. The Miniconjous and Sans Arcs led by Touch the Clouds, Red Bear, and High Bear, numbered almost a thousand. A few days later, the first small groups from Crazy Horse's camp began to arrive. Lieutenant William Philo Clark and a small contingent met Crazy Horse a few miles from the post and a ceremonial exchange of war regalia took place. For the first time since childhood, this Sioux chief met a U.S. soldier in friendship.

On May 6, 1877, Crazy Horse and his followers marched in to the Red Cloud Agency, preceded by Lieutenant Clark and Red Cloud, flanked by Little Big Man, He Dog, Little Hawk, and Big Road. The procession was two miles in length, with just under nine

---

[14] Eli Ricker's interview with William Garnett produced this information. The interview is quoted in Olson, *Red Cloud,* 237-38. The incident is also mentioned in Anderson, "Peace Talkers," 250. Hyde infers this may be so, but mentions no promises, *Red Cloud's Folk,* 290.

hundred people. Two thousand ponies and over one hundred weapons were surrendered. The two agencies of Red Cloud and Spotted Tail had seen 4500 Indians return from the hunting grounds that spring, and only one band remained outstanding: fifty-one lodges under Lame Deer.[15] These few were caught by Colonel Miles and defeated the day after Crazy Horse arrived at Camp Robinson. The Sioux were now a conquered people.

The Red Cloud Indian Agency was settled on the headwaters of the White River in northwestern Nebraska. Dr. James Irwin would be appointed agent on July 1, 1877, following the dismissal of agent James S. Hastings on July 22, 1876, in the repercussions over the Battle of the Little Big Horn, and an interim period of supervision by junior officers. The agency was stationed next to Camp Robinson, which was commanded by Lieutenant Colonel Luther P. Bradley. Also associated with the agency and military post was Lieutenant William Philo Clark, known as White Hat to the Indians, who commanded the Indian scouts and was entrusted to keep Crook fully informed as to the Indian affairs at the agency. Dr. Valentine McGillycuddy, whose correspondence appears in this work, served as assistant post surgeon at Camp Robinson.

A little more than forty miles downstream was the Spotted Tail Agency and Camp Sheridan. The major figure here was the head chief, Spotted Tail, who had the ability to develop strong positive relationships both

---

[15] Francis F. Victor, "Mountain and Frontier," *South Dakota Historical Collections,* vol. XVII, p. 312; Doane Robinson in *ibid.,* 442-43; Hyde, *Red Cloud's Folk,* 291. Several sources place the date on May 5, however Olson convincingly places the date on the 6th (p. 239).

with his people, the Brulé Sioux, and the army officers and agent. He had a close friendship with Agent Jesse M. Lee and his family, often dining with them. Camp Sheridan was commanded by Captain Daniel W. Burke.

Late in May, following the surrender of the northern bands, General Crook held a conference with several of the chiefs. The central point of discussion was the future location of the agencies. The Indians expressed adamant opposition to moving either to the Missouri River or Indian Territory. Crook had made promises of securing them an agency of their choosing in the north, and wished to send a delegation of chiefs to Washington to discuss the matter.

Rutherford Hayes had won the Presidential election of 1876 and there was hope that Crook would be successful in securing a positive policy for the Indians, as he was personally acquainted with the new president. But events of the coming summer would nurture little sympathy in Washington for the particular wishes of the Sioux agency population. There were crises elsewhere which would determine Indian policy.

The agencies remained calm on the surface throughout June and July. On July 16, Bradley wrote to Crook from Camp Robinson, "We are as quiet here as a Yankee Village on a Sunday." Two weeks later White Hat Clark wrote "Crazy Horse and his people are getting quite sociable. . ."[16] Concealed beneath the apparent calm, however, was a growing turbulence among the various camps and their chiefs.

Crazy Horse had made a favorable impression upon many at the agency in the first few days he was there. Lieutenant Bourke visited him on the first day he arrived and gave the following description of the warrior:

---

[16] Olson, *Red Cloud*, 240.

"Quite young, not over thirty years old, five feet eight inches high, lithe and sinewy, with a scar on his face. The expression of his countenance was one of quiet dignity, but morose, dogged, tenacious, and melancholy." [17] Many of the young men in the camp revered him as a great war leader who had brought glory to their people. As Bourke pointed out, "I have never heard an Indian mention his name save in terms of respect." Crazy Horse's ability to command respect extended beyond the Sioux. He also gained prestige among the army officers. And as his stature grew at the Red Cloud Agency, jealousy among the chiefs began to work its way into agency affairs.

Special Agent Benjamin R. Shapp came to the Red Cloud Agency and held a council with the chiefs on July 27. The chiefs expressed once again their opposition to being moved to the Missouri River. At the close of the meeting the growing dissension among rival chiefs broke into the open. A feast was proposed and Young Man Afraid of His Horse suggested that it be held in the Crazy Horse camp. Red Cloud and a few others promptly got up and walked out of the meeting. That night two representatives from Red Cloud came to Agent Irwin and told him that Crazy Horse had no right to hold a feast at his camp, as he was new to the reservation. Furthermore, they said, he was totally unreconstructed from his wild ways. Given the opportunity to go on a hunt the coming fall, he would surely run off and go on the warpath. [18]

On July 28, the day after Shapp's conference, Agent Irwin received notification from Crook to start issuing ammunition to the agency Indians, presumably in prep-

---

[17] Bourke, *On the Border with Crook,* 414.
[18] Olson, *Red Cloud,* 241.

aration for the hunt. Several chiefs, however, notably Spotted Tail, spoke up about the rumors of trouble brewing and warned against the hunt, causing the order to be rescinded.

Crazy Horse was becoming more and more disenchanted with his decision to surrender the previous spring. If the malicious rumors spread by rival chiefs regarding Crazy Horse's recalcitrance to the new way of life at the agency had factual basis, the reasons were quite obvious. Soon after he had arrived, he had watched the Cheyennes being marched south to Indian Territory against their will. Persistent rumors were reaching him regarding the possible forced removal of the Sioux to the Missouri River. Spotted Tail and others were speaking out against the hunt, and the issuance of ammunition had been cancelled. Now he was being approached to join a delegation to Washington to see President Hayes. He quietly refused the offer.

As the tensions grew almost imperceptibly at the White River agencies, the army's attention was drawn elsewhere by a series of crises throughout the West in the summer of 1877. There would be no time for special handling of personality differences and disenchantment among a few Sioux chiefs. Railroad workers were faced with a ten percent cut in pay, and a strike blossomed in Chicago in July. It quickly spread throughout the country and troops were called in to restore order. Crook was forced to cut the strength of the agency posts in order to deal with the strike. Apaches in the Southwest, particularly at San Carlos, were causing headaches. Most importantly to the Sioux, a small band of Nez Percés under Chief Joseph had rebelled against a forced removal from their ancestral lands in the Wallowa Valley of northeastern Oregon and were on the run, their destination unknown by the army.

Toward the end of August, Touch the Clouds, a seven-foot-tall Miniconjou chief and good friend of Crazy Horse, was called by White Hat Clark to come to the Red Cloud Agency from his camp at the Spotted Tail Agency. Clark had received orders to recruit a group of scouts from among the Sioux to aid in the capture of the Nez Percés. In consequence, a council was held at Red Cloud with Clark discussing the matter with Touch the Clouds, Crazy Horse, and several other agency chiefs. Louis Bordeaux and Frank Grouard were to interpret.[19]

Clark made an appeal to the chiefs to aid in the capture of the Nez Percés. Crazy Horse replied to the appeal through Grouard, but at the end of his speech there was a misunderstanding. According to one account, Crazy Horse told Clark that he was upset because there was no hunt, that he had thought his people were through with war after their surrender the previous spring; but if the white men wished it, he would fight until there were no Nez Percés left. Grouard somehow twisted the words, saying in his translation that Crazy Horse would fight until there were no *white* men left.[20] Only Bordeaux was immediately aware of

---

[19] For the details of this meeting and the events which followed it I have relied extensively on the account of Agent Jesse Lee given in Brininstool, *Crazy Horse,* and the *South Dakota Historical Collections,* vol. XVII, pp. 315-335.

[20] Among the many accounts which mention the misinterpretation are Dr. McGillycuddy in Brininstool, "Chief Crazy Horse, His Career and Death," 38; Louis Bordeaux in W. J. Bordeaux, *Custer's Conqueror,* (Sioux Falls, n.d.) 71; Lee's account cited in footnote 19 follows this closely, though by way of the later meeting with Touch the Clouds at Camp Sheridan; see also Sandoz, *Crazy Horse,* 392. DeBarthe, *The Life and Adventures of Frank Grouard,* (Norman, 1958) fails to make any mention of the incident.

the mistake. The council almost broke up as Grouard, Bordeaux, and the chiefs began exchanging angry words. Grouard walked out of the meeting. Perhaps Clark was more angry than anyone, as he sent for interpreter William Garnett to complete the talk. Bordeaux had withdrawn into sullen silence, and would not cooperate with him. Crazy Horse now seemed to be threatening to go on the warpath. When Garnett arrived, Crazy Horse told Clark that he would go and fight, but he wanted to take along the women and children and do a little hunting at the same time. Clark, still unaware of the misinterpretation, would have none of it. Crazy Horse and his sympathizers had had enough of talking, and left the meeting.

Touch the Clouds returned to the Spotted Tail Agency on Friday, August 31. Captain Burke had been notified by Clark the same day that recruitment of scouts for the Nez Percés campaign had been cancelled at the Red Cloud Agency, and that all northern Sioux camps were to be surrounded. Clark mentioned Touch the Clouds' refusal to cooperate with Clark regarding the Nez Percés problem and said that he expected the Miniconjou chief to bolt from the agency with his camp to join Crazy Horse at any minute. Both Burke and Agent Lee found this information hard to believe because of the cooperation and honesty of Touch the Clouds previous to this affair. A conference was called in Burke's office at Camp Sheridan with Touch the Clouds, Burke, Lee, Bordeaux, Grouard, and other agency chiefs. With Bordeaux interpreting, Touch the Clouds related the events of the council at Red Cloud. It soon became evident that Grouard had misinterpreted the speech of the chiefs in some manner. Bordeaux and Grouard once again began to argue heatedly.

Suddenly Touch the Clouds realized the mistake Grouard had made at Red Cloud. He turned to him, calling him a liar, and declaring that he (Touch the Clouds) had done all that was asked of him by the whites since he had come in the previous spring and would continue to do the same. Grouard admitted that he now believed Touch the Clouds' honesty.

On the following day, September 1, Agent Irwin called a council with Red Cloud and other trusted agency chiefs. They told him that they had been in council with Crazy Horse for several days and could do nothing to quiet him. They promised to help Irwin keep the agency under control.[21]

Jesse Lee at Spotted Tail was becoming convinced that there had been a great misunderstanding which was mushrooming into dangerous proportions. He left for the Red Cloud Agency and arrived on September 2. White Hat Clark had in the meantime relayed his fears to Colonel Bradley, who in turn wired Sheridan of the recent happenings at Red Cloud. "There is a good chance for trouble here. . ." he said, and Sheridan told him to hold tight and delay any action regarding the Nez Percés problem. Sheridan contacted Crook, who was on his way to Camp Brown on the Wind River in Wyoming to supervise operations against the Nez Percés, and sent him scooting back to Camp Robinson. He arrived on the second, simultaneously with Agent Lee.

Lee immediately went to Crook and Bradley and told them of his fears regarding the misunderstanding between Clark and the northern Sioux at the agency. He was sent to discuss the matter with Clark. Long and

---

[21] Olson, *Red Cloud*, 243.

frustrating argument had no effect on Clark's skepticism of the intentions of Crazy Horse and friends. Crook and Bradley came up during the conversation and thanked Lee for coming, for as Crook said, "I don't want to make a mistake, for it would, to the Indians, be the basest treachery to make a mistake in this matter." [22] But argue as he might, Lee's only accomplishment was to assure them of the peacefulness at the Spotted Tail Agency.

That afternoon, a council was to be held on White Clay Creek, just east of the Red Cloud Agency. Crook and Clark had asked all major chiefs of the agency to be there. Crook set out for the council grounds, but on the way was met by an Indian named Woman's Dress. William Garnett interpreting, Woman's Dress warned Crook that Crazy Horse planned to kill him and all those with him at the council. [23] The general was at first skeptical, saying that he never started somewhere that he didn't arrive, but Baptiste Pourier, a scout and friend of Garnett, vouched for Woman's Dress' honesty, and Clark further argued that it was absurd to take a risk and lose him as they had Custer. Crook turned around and returned to Camp Robinson.

Garnett carried a message to the chiefs already gathered on the White Clay from Clark. When he arrived, neither Crazy Horse or any of his band were in attendance. Garnett began to doubt the story of Woman's Dress. He quietly spread the word for certain trusted chiefs to come in to Robinson for a small council, as Clark had instructed.

---

[22] Lee's account in *South Dakota Historical Collections*, vol. xvii, p. 321.

[23] For a first hand account of this incident, see Garnett, herein.

A private conference was held in Colonel Bradley's office, with the friendly chiefs arguing for and supporting the subjugation of Crazy Horse. Some suggested his death. Crook could not approve such a blatant murder plot, but told Bradley to arrange for Crazy Horse's arrest and detention. He left again for Camp Brown in Wyoming that evening, trusting that his subordinates could effectively control the situation.

Unknown to Agent Lee, Spotted Tail had been sent for and he arrived at Camp Robinson on September 3 as preparations were being made for the surrounding of Crazy Horse's camp and his arrest. Lee immediately asked Bradley's permission to return to his agency with Spotted Tail in order to have some control over affairs there. Lee's last words to Clark were to be careful not to let Crazy Horse escape to his agency on Beaver Creek. Clark assured him that there was no danger, that he could arrest Crazy Horse whenever he wanted, with the aid of his spies in the camps.

Clark's assurance proved unwarranted. Early the next morning, September 4, he gathered together his troops and Indian volunteers and headed out toward Crazy Horse's camp.[24] They arrived ready to make their arrest, only to find that the camp had broken up, some of the people running in to the agency, some head-

---

[24] Among those leading their warriors in this mission were Red Cloud, Little Wound, American Horse, Young Man Afraid of His Horse, Yellow Road, Little Big Man, Big Road, and Jumping Shield. The latter three were members of Crazy Horse's own camp. Major Julius Mason led eight companies of the Third Cavalry. He is mistakenly identified as Lt. Col. John S. Mason in Olson, *Red Cloud*, 244. For the details of this march on the Crazy Horse camp the source utilized primarily is Bradley's account found in Bourke, *On the Border with Crook*, 421.

ing north, and Crazy Horse setting out alone, with his ailing wife, for the Spotted Tail Agency.[25]

Clark sent a small contingent of Indians after Crazy Horse, and then hurried into the post to make plans dealing with the unexpected turn of events. Late that Tuesday afternoon, Crazy Horse rode into the northern Sioux's camp at Spotted Tail with his wife. Burke sent for him, and he was escorted to Camp Sheridan by Touch the Clouds and several others. Spotted Tail then made a speech to Crazy Horse in front of all those gathered at the post. He was chief at his agency, Spotted Tail said, and if Crazy Horse wished to remain there, he would have to obey him. Crazy Horse was taken to Burke's office where he gave his word to return to the Red Cloud Agency the next day.

But the coming of the sun on Wednesday, September 5, brought fearful premonitions to Crazy Horse, and he asked to be allowed to stay at the Brulé agency, and have someone else go upstream to talk for him. Burke and Lee could not oblige him, but made promises regarding his safe keeping. First of all, both Lee and Crazy Horse agreed to take no weapons with them. Lee promised to tell Bradley of all that had occurred at Spotted Tail, and to say that Burke and Spotted Tail had agreed to Crazy Horse's transfer to their agency if that was what he desired. Crazy Horse was told that he could tell his side of the story covering the past few

---

[25] Some accounts say Crazy Horse first headed north, then turned back and headed downstream to the Spotted Tail Agency, as expressed in Hyde, *Red Cloud's Folk,* 297. Another account claims he headed to Spotted Tail to get medical assistance for his wife. See Vestal, *Warpath and Council Fire* (N.Y., 1948), 296. Though McGillycuddy is singled out as the doctor in question in that account, the surgeon was stationed at Red Cloud, and he personally makes no mention of this situation in any of the writings I have seen.

days in order to clear up the confusion regarding his intentions.[26]

Lee and Crazy Horse started for the Red Cloud Agency that morning. Accompanying them were Louis Bordeaux, the interpreter; Black Crow, Swift Bear, and a few other trusted agency chiefs; High Bear and Touch the Clouds, two close friends of Crazy Horse; and seven northern Sioux, sympathetic to the Oglala warrior. When they were but a few miles out from Camp Robinson, Lee sent a message to Clark informing him of the promises they made to Crazy Horse and asked where to take him when they arrived. Clark returned a note through a carrier which stated simply, "General Bradley wishes you to drive direct to his office with Crazy Horse, Yours, Clark." When they arrived at the adjutant's office at the military post, they were informed that Crazy Horse was to be turned over to Captain Kennington, the officer of the day.

Lee objected and went immediately to Bradley. He explained the promises that he and Burke had made that morning to Crazy Horse, but Bradley had his orders, and was a man who followed them to the letter. Crazy Horse was to be arrested and confined. He was subsequently to be shipped to Omaha where he could be held out of harm's way until he could be removed to some distant location.[27]

Crazy Horse was consequently led toward the guard

---

[26] Lee's account in Brininstool, *Crazy Horse*, 29.

[27] Bradley stated that his orders from Crook were to send Crazy Horse to Omaha, while Crook notified Sheridan that Bradley was sending the warrior to him in Cheyenne. See Olson, *Red Cloud*, 244. Lee heard from a second-hand source in the Third Cavalry that Crazy Horse's eventual destination was to be Dry Tortugas, Florida. See Brininstool, *Crazy Horse*, 34. McGillycuddy repeats this rumor in *ibid.*, 48.

house by a small escort of Indian police, scouts, and troops. A scuffle took place either just inside the door, or before he entered, and the warrior received a mortal wound. The eye-witness accounts vary considerably regarding the specifics, as shown in the accounts herein; and as in all events of high drama, people saw what they wanted to see and reported it with their personal biases. Most say the wound was caused by a bayonet held by an army guard, as expressed by Mr. Friswold. Little Big Man, who held Crazy Horse's arms at the doorway and was wounded with Crazy Horse's knife, told Bourke at the Sun Dance in 1881 that he had accidentally deflected the knife, causing Crazy Horse to stab himself. He told Bourke that the bayonet had hit the guard house door, and that the marks it had left could still be seen. Fear of revenge, apparently, had prevented him from revealing his knowledge of the events.[28] Several others stated that the doctor could not determine whether the wound was from a bayonet or knife.[29] McGillycuddy, the surgeon who examined Crazy Horse and stayed with him that night, makes no such allusion to doubt regarding the instrument causing the wound, specifying the bayonet.[30]

Crazy Horse was taken to the adjutant's office where he died that night. His body was turned over to his mother and father, who later disposed of his bones in secrecy. His ailing wife died a few days later.[31] Things remained under control on the agencies. Clark reported that the Indians felt Crazy Horse had brought death on

[28] Bourke, *On the Border with Crook,* 422.

[29] Quoting Bradley from Olson, *Red Cloud,* 245.

[30] Julia B. McGillycuddy, *McGillycuddy, Agent,* 92; and McGillycuddy in Brininstool, *Crazy Horse,* 45.

[31] Lee's diary entry of September 13, 1877, in Brininstool, *Crazy Horse,* 40.

himself by drawing the knife at the guard house. The feared conflicts which might have resulted from the warrior's death failed to materialize.

Within a month's time a delegation of chiefs was sent to Washington to meet with President Hayes. Among the most well-known were Red Cloud, Spotted Tail, American Horse, Young Man Afraid of His Horse, He Dog, and Little Big Man. General Crook and Lieutenant Clark were also in attendance. At this conference the chiefs once again expressed opposition to any move east to the Missouri River. In spite of their pleas and anger, the coming of winter saw them moving slowly downstream from the Red Cloud and Spotted Tail agencies toward their new locations on the Missouri. They had been starved out, as contracts for supply shipments designated the Missouri River agencies as final destination, and the army refused to move the goods further west.

A few bands of northern Sioux broke from the column and headed north in search of freedom. Red Cloud and Spotted Tail both halted their camps on the White River, many miles upstream from the new agencies, and refused to budge. Agent Irwin and others finally raised such a fuss that the supplies were moved west. The military fumed at the exorbitant rates the teamsters charged.

The following summer of 1878 Red Cloud and Spotted Tail once again moved, this time to their final destinations. Red Cloud settled on what was to be the Pine Ridge Agency, not far from the old Spotted Tail Agency on Beaver Creek. Spotted Tail settled at the Rosebud Agency, over 150 miles west of the Missouri below the White River. Both moved without authorization because of bureaucratic manipulation which was hampering action at the time in the Indian Bureau.

## The Killing of Chief Crazy Horse

Fears that some of the Sioux might join renegade Cheyenne in raids and killing did not materialize. The Cheyenne had made a daring escape from a miserable existence in Indian Territory and dashed north to the abandoned Red Cloud Agency, cautiously dodging a variety of pursuers. After much suffering, they were allowed to stay with their allies at the new South Dakota agencies.

Agent Irwin resigned his post in January 1879, addressing a scathing letter to Commissioner of Indian Affairs, Ezra H. Hayt, in which he stated his disgust with Hayt's management of affairs in the Bureau and condemned his "crude and impracticable theories" so dogmatically adhered to.[32] Dr. Valentine McGillycuddy was appointed his replacement at Pine Ridge. The Sioux had become an agency-bound people, and the reality, if not the memory, of the days of the hunt and lodge was now, together with Crazy Horse, completely lost.

ROBERT A. CLARK

---

[32] Olson, *Red Cloud,* 264.

# History of Chief Crazy Horse
## by Chief He Dog

CHIEF CRAZY HORSE

CHIEF HE DOG, 1837-1936
Mr. Fred Hackett, who knew the Chief, says he was a
short, heavily-built, powerful man with tremendous
vitality and a keen sense of humor. He learned to speak
fairly good English. He was shrewd, a ferocious fighter,
and a loyal friend to Crazy Horse.

# Portrait of Chief Crazy Horse

Herein is an enlargement of what I believe is an authentic picture of Crazy Horse. The original is a small tintype, 2½ x 3½ inches, in excellent condition. Its first owner was Baptiste Garnier (Little Bat) the famous scout and frontiersman. When Bat was murdered in 1900 it went to his wife; on her death it was inherited by her daughter, Ellen Howard, from whom Mr. Hackett obtained it, after which it came to me, so the line of ownership is quite clear. I have a certificate from Mrs. Howard attesting that the tintype belonged to her father, and that it had been in the family since it had been made. She also says that her father told his family it was truly a picture of Crazy Horse.

First publication was by J. W. Vaughn in his excellent *With Crook at the Rosebud,* (Stackpole, 1956). The account tells of finding the picture in an old trunk, which is probably true, but after that point my investigations do not agree with the information supplied to Mr. Vaughn. The account said the picture was taken about 1870 at Fort Laramie. There were two other pictures, one of Little Bat and his wife, and the other of Bat and Frank Grouard. We do not know if they were part of the same series but if they were, they were not taken in 1870 for the following reasons: Grouard tells in his biography, *Life and Adventures of Frank Grouard,* by Joe DeBarthe (1894, p. 117), that he met Crazy Horse for the first time just a few days after the battle between the Sioux and the Stanley Expedition on the Yellowstone River – this took place August 4th, 1873. Another point, in 1870 Bat was 15 or 16 years old;

## The Killing of Chief Crazy Horse

I do not believe a war chief of the Oglalas was hanging around with a teen-ager. Crazy Horse had been made a chief only a little more than a year previous – he was out in the hinterlands with his bands of warriors and their families; he was not hanging around the fort for the white man's handouts as did Red Cloud and Spotted Tail. At this time and for several more years probably his only contact with the white man was across the sights of his Winchester.

Following their surrender in May 1877, Crazy Horse and his chief warriors were signed up as Indian Scouts ostensibly to keep tab on the Nez Percé, but with Lieutenant Clark on the job you may be sure they were under his eagle eye both day and night. The whites were afraid of this man and kept close track of his every move, so he was not let out on any scouting trips. Time was very heavy on his hands, the tiny details of every day living were a nuisance to him, begging for supplies and food, or settling a quarrel between the women, so one day when Little Bat rode past the camp on his way to Fort Robinson he easily persuaded Crazy Horse to come along just to see what they could see. Crazy Horse liked Bat, and Mrs. Bat was a cousin of his, so he was at ease and relaxed, being with his friends. While at the Fort, with everyone in high good humor Bat dared Crazy Horse to have his picture taken, and he finally consented. According to the story he even borrowed the moccasins to make a good appearance. I know all previous picture requests had been refused; these had all been made by white men, and the white man had been trying for years to kill Crazy Horse and his people, so why should he do even the slightest favor for them. Also, on this last summer of his life he did a number of things he had never done before. On this one time he let down his guard for his good friend Bat. We also know there was a photographer at the Fort in the summer of 1877 as I have another photo stamped Fort Robinson in the mounting and this was taken in 1877.

The picture shows an Indian of medium stature, lighter-haired than the average Indian, with a rounded face rather than one with high, wide cheekbones. His hair is in braids to his waist, and he wears two feathers which was customary with Crazy Horse. Mr. Hackett has a set of feathers given him by an old chief and they are exactly similar to those shown in the photo. Also the picture shows clearly the scar in the left corner of his mouth where he was shot some years before by No Water, after he had ridden away with No Water's wife.

It is most unfortunate that the secretive nature of the old-time Indians dealing with whites caused this picture to be so long hidden. We know of trunks and bags which still hold relics of the Custer battle. Even thirty years ago would have been sufficient for proper identification, as He Dog lived until 1936, and Doctor McGillycuddy who knew and liked Crazy Horse, lived until June of 1939. Either man could have said yes or no at first glimpse, but neither saw it and now it is too late. From the people involved and my searches I firmly believe this is an authentic likeness of Crazy Horse.

CARROLL FRISWOLD

# History of Chief Crazy Horse
## by Chief He Dog
### as written down by his son
### Rev. Eagle Hawk, Oglala, S. Dak.

In order to be made a chief of this tribe of Indians, a man must observe and keep these four rules:
1. He must be brave and out-spoken.
2. He must be ambitious.
3. He must be honest at all times.
4. He must be kind to all creatures.

Any Indian wishing to be made a chief must observe and strictly obey these main four rules.

After a person has become a chief, he receives the following:
1. A beaded buckskin outfit.
2. An eagle fether to wear in his hair.
3. A pipe and tobacco bags.

After being given these things he is given a lecture on the subject of the responsibilities he will acquire as a chief. This lecture is given by one of the wise old men of the tribe. After he is made a chief and he later fails to obey the four rules stated above or commits a crime against his people, he is made to drink the oil taken from a dog. This is administered by a sort of policeman of the tribe. By doing this, it is hoped that the evil things will be washed out of him. It is an Indian custom. If he does anything seriously wrong again, he is deprived of his chief's clothing and ordered out of the tribe for five years.

After the five years he is given another chance to

become a chief. The five years is given as a punishment and time to acquire experience. If, after being made a chief the second time, he still insists on being bad, he is not only ordered out of the tribe for good; but, as the saying goes, his ears and tail are cut off and he has to live as a wolf without its ears and tail. This is another custom of the Oglala Sioux.

Anyone who is made a chief, may be a chief for as long as he may live and conduct himself as he should.

When a man is made a chief, he is lectured, also, on these different points:

1. He should remember that there are a lot of wasps and flies that sting, and beware lest they sting and confuse him.
2. He should remember that there are a lot of dogs that will bark and defile his tent or place of dwelling, but he shouldn't pay any attention to the dogs.
3. If one of his close kin is killed in battle, he must not stop to look, lest he feel the need to retaliate. It is considered disgraceful for him to lose his temper.
4. He must not be stingy with his food. He must feed everyone that may visit him.
5. He must offer tobacco to whomever visits him.

Long ago, the tribe was his responsibility.

The men listed below were made chiefs and were the best:

1. Chief Red Cloud
2. Chief Afraid of Horse
3. Chief Red Dog
4. Chief Little Wound
5. Chief Spotted Face
6. Chief Smoke
7. Chief Wounded Face
8. Chief Fast Whirlwind
9. Chief Bushy Hair
10. Chief Fire Thunder

These were all old chiefs of the Oglala Sioux Tribe. There were many, but these were the main leaders.

These old chiefs held a council and decided to elect new and younger men to be chiefs. The men selected were to be out of the committee men or committee workers. There were five young men selected to replace the old chiefs. They were as follows:

1. Crazy Horse
2. He Dog
3. Young Man Afraid of His Horses
4. American Horse
5. Carries Sword

Chief's clothing, pipes, and tobacco pouches were made for them. One day a big council was held to make these men chiefs. These men pledged the chief's oath, and were given the chief's clothing, pipes, and tobacco pouches. They were made to smoke the pipes to show their good faith.

After these men were made chiefs, the Oglala Sioux Tribe broke up into two groups as a result of discord among the leaders or chiefs. Most of the old chiefs left with Chief Red Cloud and moved from place to place, finally going to Fort Robinson in the state of Nebraska. Crazy Horse and his group stayed up north.

After settling at Fort Robinson, Chiefs Red Cloud, He Dog, and others went to try to bring Crazy Horse and his group to Fort Robinson, to live among the white men in peace. They took gifts of tobacco, food, blankets, etc., to Chief Crazy Horse. He agreed to go back with them to Fort Robinson. Chief Red Cloud and his group were living in peace with the white men, learning their language and ways of life. Chief Red Cloud's group asked the rest of the Sioux people to live with them in peace, too. This was after the fight with General George Custer's forces. The United States wanted the Indians put on reservations. Therefore, Red Cloud's group was sent out from Fort Robinson to attempt to make peace with Chief Crazy Horse, while he was camped at what is known as Powder Creek, somewhere in Montana.

## The Killing of Chief Crazy Horse

After the arrival of Chief Red Cloud and his band, a lot of tents were pitched together. One large tent was pitched in the middle of the village. A big council was to be held in that one. After the council got under way, a lot of people were there. Chief Crazy Horse stood up and asked Chief Red Cloud the purpose of his call or visit. One of the leaders of Red Cloud's group stood up to answer. He said, "Before we tell you the reason why we come to you from such a long way, we wish to present to you some gifts that we have brought with us. We have horses, blankets, tobacco, food, sugar, and candy for Chief Crazy Horse and Chief He Dog, who are the leaders of their groups. To each we present a horse, pack of food, blanket and clothing."

After the gifts were presented, the man said that Chief Red Cloud and the President of the United States talked together. Red Cloud was sent by the President of the United States to try and get Chiefs Crazy Horse and He Dog to lay down their arms and come back to a reservation that had been set aside for them, to live in peace and shed no more blood.

Crazy Horse and He Dog stood up to speak. They said, "It is a long way from where you came and we know how hard it must have been on you to make that journey. But we are very glad that you have come and so we extend to you and your group a hearty welcome and we shall answer you."

He Dog spoke and he said, "We and other Indians were born and raised on this land. The Great Spirit of God gave us this land. He created animals which we catch and make clothing and shelter for our people, and also the sweets that grow on trees. God gave us this land to live on and protect as our own. You know what the Great White Father and his soldiers do to us? They make war, burn our homes, our tents, wherever we may be and kill our people. It is only right that we protect ourselves, our people, and our country. The only thing we can do is protect ourselves and fight with the soldiers. We do not fight because we want to, but because we have to, to stay alive. We do not want to spill blood, either ours or the white man's. Therefore, we agree with you. We will go back with you to live in peace with the white men, and learn their ways."

After Chief Crazy Horse and Chief He Dog sat down, there was clapping of hands and grunts of approval from the old men of the tribe.

Chief Crazy Horse and Chief He Dog stood up again to speak further. They said, "We agree to go back with you, but you, Red Cloud, with your group, will leave first; and when you get back to Fort Robinson, tell the Great White Father's soldiers' leader that we are coming back but that it will be a slow journey, because of the old people and children. There are so many in our group." Chief Red Cloud said that he would do that.

So the journey back to Fort Robinson started. Chief Red Cloud's group left first and then Crazy Horse and He Dog's groups left later. They camped at night along the way. It was a long and slow journey.

Somewhere along the way, they were camped in a valley, when Chief He Dog walked up a hill and sat down, looking down at the camp where Chief Crazy Horse was. After a while, Crazy Horse came up to him and said, "I just came up to talk with you about something. Tomorrow, Lame Deer and his band plan to go back the way we came. They are going to hunt for buffalo once more and I plan to go back with them."

Chief He Dog answered, saying, "You think like a

child. You smoked the pipe of peace the same as I. You promised to go back with Chief Red Cloud and to live in peace with the white men. Don't run away from our grandfathers. Do not do it. It is not good." But Crazy Horse said nothing.

The next morning, Chief Crazy Horse left with Chief Lame Deer's band to go back north to hunt for buffalo. But the rest of the group left in the direction of Fort Robinson. After traveling many days, Chief He Dog's group made camp. Then he was informed that Chief Crazy Horse had returned again to his group, so they traveled on.

One day they met Chief Red Cloud's band with a detachment of cavalry from Fort Robinson coming back to meet them. The Indians made their camp in a circle to talk. Chief Crazy Horse made his camp opposite to that of Chief He Dog. The detachment of soldiers rode around the camp and stopped in front of Chief He Dog's tent. The officer in charge of the soldiers and the interpreter got off their horses. The officer was known as White Hat to the Indians and the interpreter was called Blaila. They greeted Chief He Dog and shook hands with him. The soldiers had stopped at Chief Crazy Horse's tent before they came to He Dog's tent, but Chief Crazy Horse did not greet them. The officer said to Chief He Dog, "We stopped at Chief Crazy Horse's tent, but he didn't greet us, not even as much as to nod to us. You have greeted us warmly and for that I am happy. I have heard about you two chiefs up north, you and Crazy Horse. They say you were like two fires in the night. Now that I have seen you, you are both small in stature and big in name. I am happy that I have met you both. No matter how fierce or brave a person thinks he is, if he learns to humble himself once in a while, he will be well liked, and good things will happen to him. Also, think about this, Chief He Dog. The Great White Father's soldiers want two or four things from you."

Chief He Dog then asked the interpreter what the officer meant by two or four things they wanted from him. The officer and the interpreter would not tell him. They told him to think, and try to figure it out. Chief He Dog could not, so he felt bad. He talked with Chief Crazy Horse, and they thought together, but couldn't figure what it was. Chief Crazy Horse asked Chief He Dog to arrange a council with Chief Red Cloud, ask Spoon Woman's permission, and ask Chief Deer Antler to be there also.

At the meeting, Chiefs Crazy Horse and He Dog asked Chief Red Cloud if he knew what the officer meant when he said that they wanted two or four things from them. Chief Red Cloud said that he did not know either. Then the meeting broke up.

The next morning the group resumed the journey toward Fort Robinson. Chiefs Crazy Horse and He Dog stayed behind, after everyone had left, still trying to figure out what the army officer meant when he said that he wanted two or four things from them. Failing in that, they took out the pipe and prayed to the Holy Spirit to tell them what it was that the soldiers wanted from them. They had two saddle horses that they were going to ride back to join the group. But the horses wandered away, leaving them afoot. They had to walk to the next camp.

When White Hat first greeted Chief He Dog, he gave him a square piece of white cloth, saying, "The next time we come I will be in the lead. When we stop at your tepee, you will pin this white piece of cloth to my left shoulder."

The next morning, as the journey was resumed, they

met a detachment of cavalry with White Hat in the lead. Chief He Dog remembered what he was supposed to do with the piece of white cloth that the officer had given him. So when they met, he got off his horse and walked up to the officer, who had also dismounted, and tied the piece of white cloth to the officer's left shoulder. White Hat said to He Dog, "You have done what I asked you to do. For that, I am very happy. We have brought you some food and fresh beef. It is coming in the wagons."

"I will tell you what we will do tomorrow. Tomorrow, before we reach Fort Robinson, we will stop and make camp. We will hold a big council to make peace. This will be for my people and yours. After I leave, inform your people what I have said. There will be a lot of soldiers there for the big council meeting." Then White Hat left with his soldiers. Chief He Dog informed his people what White Hat had said.

The journey was resumed at noon the next day. They met the soldiers coming to meet them. Camp was made and preparations were made for the big council. A lot of soldiers were there besides the Indians. All the soldiers were on one side, and the Indians were on the opposite side. They were facing each other. In the middle of the two groups were Chief Red Cloud, Chief He Dog, Chief Crazy Horse, and the army officer, White Hat.

When the council started, Chief He Dog thought he knew what it was that the soldiers wanted of them. When the Sioux fought with General Custer at the Little Big Horn in Montana, all the soldiers were killed. Some of He Dog's band took the soldier's horses and they still had some of these horses with them. He Dog traded two of his own horses for an army horse, saddle, bridle, etc. that an old man had. They were in his possession when the big council got under way.

Chief He Dog brought out the army horse with the saddle, revolver, rifle, and also his personal war equipment, and his warbonnet. This warbonnet, he placed on officer White Hat's head, saying, "These things are yours. The horse, saddle, the revolver, and the rifle, I give them back to you." Chief Crazy Horse gave Chief Red Cloud a horse, and a buffalo robe with porcupine quills.

Chief He Dog spoke, saying, "It is a very nice day. I am glad that we meet again. I offer a handshake in honor of this occasion of our coming to make peace. We must make it strong and lasting. The Great Spirit above wishes us to lay down our arms to live in peace, to make war no more. Looking back in the past, the land or earth is big, half of it is yours and half is ours. We have fought each other. Your soldiers and my people see the bones of horses and men. The blood of men has been spilled. We have caused it, you and I. On this day we will bury days. The blood that we have spilled we will forget. The wars that we have fought, we shall never fight again. To the honor of our good intentions to make peace," – Chief He Dog gave the pipe filled with tobacco to the army officer – "when I raise both arms to the sky, you will put the pipe to your mouth." When Chief He Dog raised both arms to the sky, White Hat put the pipe in his mouth. Chief He Dog began to pray to the Great Spirit, and White Hat also prayed.

After this, Chief He Dog said, "We will return to you all the army rifles that we have in our possession. They belong to you. The Great White Father made them for us to fight each other. So I will return them to you this day." Chief He Dog shook White Hat's hand and put one arm around his neck and hugged him.

57

## The Killing of Chief Crazy Horse

Chief Crazy Horse spoke saying just about the same as Chief He Dog said to the army officer, White Hat, only he spoke to Chief Red Cloud. He said, "I give you, Chief Red Cloud, all my horses, and the old people and children shall take care of them as your own." And then Chief Crazy Horse shook hands with Chief Red Cloud and hugged him also.

Chief Red Cloud spoke, saying, "I will do what you have told me." Then he clasped Chief Crazy Horse's hand. After this, everyone started shaking hands and greeting each other in a friendly fashion.

White Hat spoke, saying, "I will tell you what you must do tomorrow. Chief He Dog and Chief Crazy Horse, tomorrow, we will reach Fort Robinson. I am informing you that there are four important buildings that you must enter in Fort Robinson. There is the fort, the Commanding Army's base; the Agency Superintendent's house; the church; and the agency trader's store. You must decide which of these buildings you must enter first."

Chief He Dog and Crazy Horse told White Hat, "We will go, but we don't know which building we must enter first. You must know which we should enter first. Would you tell us?"

White Hat said, "You are not children anymore. You can think for yourselves."

The next morning, the journey to Fort Robinson began with Chief Crazy Horse and Chief He Dog in the lead of their group on horses. When they arrived at Fort Robinson, they stopped to think which building to enter first. Chief He Dog said, "Let's go to the church first." Chief Crazy Horse said, "Let's go to the sutler's store first. Then we can go to the others last." They decided to go to the store first, got an interpreter, and talked to the store owner. They told him what the army officer had said. Then they went to the other places. The Agency Superintendent told them where to live. Later they went down to White River and came upon the Indian camp grounds and started to build their camps. While in that process some soldiers rounded up all the Indian horses. There were several hundred, and they drove them away. Some other soldiers gathered up all the Indians' rifles and stacked them all in one place.

All the Indians gathered around where the soldiers had stacked the rifles. The commanding officer, all the important people of the fort, and the friendly Indians were there. The commanding officer spoke to Chief Crazy Horse, Chief He Dog, and their group. Chief Red Cloud, Chief Spotted Tail, and their tribes were all present. The commanding officer said, "Chief Crazy Horse and Chief He Dog, you have been fighting up north, but you have come to Fort Robinson with Chief Red Cloud. I asked you for your horses and guns, and you turned them over to me willingly. I wish to thank you and welcome you in a manner befitting the Great White Father's soldiers. I will give you your horses back, but I will keep your rifles." Chief Crazy Horse and He Dog said, "How," meaning that they agreed.

Chief Red Cloud spoke next, saying about the same as the commanding officer. He said it was a good thing to turn over their horses and guns. He said he was glad the army officers would return the horses. And he said, "There is one thing they want you to do. Chief Crazy Horse and Chief He Dog, the army wants you to go to the Great White Father, and make your peace with him officially. I am told that you and your tribes will be given a place to live, wherever you choose. You can live in the Black Hills, if you will go to Washington and make your peace with him." Chief Crazy Horse would be the sole chief for the tribe. The other chiefs already there were jealous of Chief Crazy Horse because he was an important chief.

That evening, the people of Chief Crazy Horse and Chief He Dog visited the tepees of the Indians there, including Chiefs Red Cloud, Spotted Tail, American Horse, Young Man Afraid of His Horses, and many others. Some of them were related and hadn't seen each other for a long time. There was some crying as well as happy greetings. They exchanged gifts of food, clothing, and other things.

One day Chief Crazy Horse and Chief He Dog's groups separated because of some disagreement. A short while after this, Chief He Dog was made a scout by the officer commanding Fort Robinson.

One day Chief He Dog was told to tell Chief Crazy Horse that they were to get ready to go to Washington that day. He Dog went to tell Crazy Horse, but Crazy Horse wasn't home. Several times Chief He Dog was told to tell Chief Crazy Horse to get ready to go to Washington, but Chief Crazy Horse was either not home, or he would make some kind of excuse not to go.

He Dog went again to see Chief Crazy Horse, but he wasn't home. Chief Crazy Horse's father called his son and told him that he had a visitor. Crazy Horse came back with his father to the tepee, and asked Chief He Dog what he wanted. He Dog said, "These people have been telling you not to go to Washington because the army will kill you. It's not true, whatever they tell you. Do not believe them. They lie. They are jealous of you. I'm telling you that you should go with me."

Chief Crazy Horse said, "Two white men came to see me a while ago. They gave me two pocket knives, with the blades open. They shook my hand." He went into the tepee and took the two knives from under his pillow and showed them to He Dog. One was red and the other blue. Crazy Horse said, "The two white men who gave me the knives wore grey clothes. They told me they were army officers but since they were not in uniform I didn't think they were army men."

Chief He Dog said, "I never said that they never told you to cross White River. These people have been saying that about me since you have refused to go to Washington with me. Maybe they meant these two knives as a bad sign of something to come. I don't know." He laughed.

Chief Crazy Horse said that he would go with Chief He Dog to Washington. Chief He Dog went back and told the army officer and then went home to his camp at a place called Spring Creek.

A short while after, some of Chief Crazy Horse's people came to Chief He Dog's camp, singing and standing in single file. The leader of the group was riding a grey horse, and told He Dog that Crazy Horse sent them to bring him and his group back to Chief Crazy Horse's camp. He Dog refused, so they returned.

Sometime later a scout was sent to He Dog's village and informed him that he was wanted at a meeting in Chief Red Cloud's village. He left that night for Chief Red Cloud's place. When he got there, he paused to listen outside of the meeting place. And he heard them discussing guns and ammunition. He listened a while before he went in. They seemed to be discussing Chief Crazy Horse. As he entered, he was greeted with "How's" from all who were there. He asked them, "What is the purpose of this meeting, and why do you wish my presence?"

He was told it concerned Chief Crazy Horse. The soldiers were to go after him the next morning. They said they were after two types of guns from him. The soldiers anticipated trouble from Chief Crazy Horse's people, so that is why they were told to prepare guns and ammunition. He Dog asked them when they were going after Chief Crazy Horse. They told him that the soldiers and scouts were going after him early next morning.

The meeting lasted all night, and at dawn the soldiers and scouts arrived at the meeting place. The army officer in charge told them what they should do. He said there would be three groups going to Chief Crazy Horse's camp in three different directions. In the center group would be Chief He Dog, and American Horse and their groups. The group arriving from the north would be Chief Afraid of His Horses with soldiers and scouts. The group coming up on the south side would be Three Bear's chief scout, his scouts, and soldiers.

After this, they moved out as directed, when some Indian identified as Crazy Bear, one of Chief Crazy Horse's men, rode up from the direction of the Fort, shouting, "It's bad! It's going to be bad!" He rode past the group of soldiers, scouts, and Indians on his way back to Crazy Horse's camp. It was assumed that he informed Chief Crazy Horse of what had happened. When Chief Crazy Horse's people heard about it, they were fearful for their chief. They gathered in groups, discussing the situation.

Meanwhile, the soldiers, scouts, and Indians were advancing toward Chief Crazy Horse's village. As they were nearing a hill, a rider came over the hill, waving a revolver in the air. The line of soldiers, scouts, and Indians stopped, but the rider turned around and headed back the way he had come from Chief Crazy Horse's camp. Someone identified the rider as a young boy named Matukna, showing off, so they continued on their way. Another rider rode up, identified as Looking Horse, one of Chief Crazy Horse's warriors. He had on an eagle feather headdress. He came up to the line of soldiers, scouts, and Indians, and rode back and forth in front of them, saying to the scouts and Indians, "You are Indians, too. Why do you take the side of the white man against Chief Crazy Horse and his people?" He called them all kinds of names and showed his contempt for them.

An Indian scout in the group, named Buffalo Dance, shouted, "When I bring soldiers anywhere, I don't want anyone to talk to me that way!" And he shot the warrior Looking Horse's horse out from under him. Another scout rode up to the unhorsed warrior and pistol-whipped him. A scout named White Cow Killer, a brother of the warrior, Looking Horse, said, "Look what they did to you as a result!" He half carried and half dragged him beneath a tree, and put his saddle blanket for a pillow.

The group continued on towards Crazy Horse's camp, when another rider met them, so they stopped. The rider, identified as Black Fox, one of Chief Crazy Horse's closest allies, had on a warbonnet, and was riding a fine buckskin pony. Black Fox said to them, "Is Chief He Dog and American Horse in this group?" Chief He Dog and American Horse said they were. Black Fox said, "Let's dismount and have a smoke. Even a man about to die takes time to smoke." While the rest of the group waited, the three of them sat down to smoke, Black Fox sitting between the two chiefs. The two chiefs noticed that he carried a knife in a sheath around his waist, besides the rifle he had. He watched that Black Fox might try to use the knife on them. After he had finished smoking, Black Fox said to them, "Chief Crazy Horse left last night with his wife in the direction of Chief Spotted Tail's camp. I heard you were looking for him, so I thought I would tell you."

## The Killing of Chief Crazy Horse

This information was passed on to the army officer, who ordered the buglers to sound recall, calling the other two groups of soldiers and Indians to his position. After awhile the other two groups joined his group. Several scouts were sent to Chief Spotted Tail's camp to verify the information, while the main body of soldiers and Indians returned to Fort Robinson and the villages.

Meanwhile, Chief Spotted Tail learned of Chief Crazy Horse's presence in his village and immediately he called for a meeting, requesting Chief Crazy Horse to be present. At the meeting, Chief Spotted Tail said to Chief Crazy Horse, "My brother, you have roamed like a fire in the north. You are of the Oglala. The Oglala people are yours. Something good should happen to you with them. Instead, you have run away like a wolf with its tail between its legs. This is my tribe here. I do not want anything bad to happen to you here. Therefore, I give you a fine horse as a gift. I want you to take this horse and go back to your people, the Oglalas. You will listen to me and do as I say. Some of my head men or chiefs will accompany you back to your people as soon as possible."

Chief Crazy Horse said, "I will do what you suggest."

So some of Chief Spotted Tail's chiefs started back to Chief Crazy Horse's camp with Chief Crazy Horse and his wife. On the way, they were observed by the soldiers some distance from the Fort. Other Indians watched them, too, as they were passing by Fort Robinson. A buggy with yellow wheels came out of the Fort with a white team and moved up in front of this group of Indians, with Chief Crazy Horse in the lead. Behind him followed some of Chief Spotted Tail's men.

An interpreter known as Blaila told the other Indians

that no one was to go near or talk to Chief Crazy Horse. Nevertheless, Chief He Dog rode up to Chief Crazy Horse and shook his hand and said, "You should have listened to me and we could have gone to Washington. I warned you that something like this would happen, and instead you listened to your people lie. Now, not even one of them is here to help you. You are not even with friends except me. Do you have any weapons on you?" Chief Crazy Horse said, "How."

There was a high fence all around the Fort, with one main gate. At that entrance were soldiers and scouts waiting and watching this group of buggy and horsemen. The group stopped at the entrance and the Indians all dismounted and tied their horses at the fence beside the main entrance to the fort. The soldiers took Crazy Horse inside while this was happening. Chief He Dog also rode up and tied his horse at the fence and went inside the fort. They were leading Chief Crazy Horse towards the fort's jail. But at the entrance of the building, Crazy Horse saw that it was a jail and said, "So you have been intending to put me in jail all along," and drew a knife from beneath his blanket. A small Indian named Whirlwind Bear grabbed Chief Crazy Horse. A soldier stood behind him, saying, "Whoa!" Whirlwind Bear kept saying to Crazy Horse, "Don't do that, don't do that!" Suddenly Whirlwind Bear let go of Chief Crazy Horse, and said, "He stabbed. He stabbed me!" Chief Crazy Horse's blanket fell off of him and a revolver which he had concealed, dropped. A scout named Plenty Wolves ran up and grabbed the revolver, shouting, "Hurry, I've got his gun!"

A soldier on duty with a rifle and a fixed bayonet ran up to where the scuffle was going on and waved the bayonetted rifle at them. Whirlwind Bear and the other soldier let Chief Crazy Horse go. They had been going around in circles. When they let him go, Crazy Horse fell backwards, stabbed in the back.

Chief He Dog came up just as this was happening. When he saw a man named Shoe Lace about to shoot Chief Crazy Horse while he was down, He Dog angrily told him to get away from there. The man stepped back out of the way.

Chief He Dog got his blanket and made a bed for Chief Crazy Horse and started to cover him when Crazy Horse asked him to look at his wound. He Dog looked at the wound in his back. He saw a cut on the right side of Crazy Horse's back and a little below it was a smaller deep wound with blood dripping out of it. Blood was also coming out of his mouth while he was grunting, more from anger than from pain. Chief He Dog laid him down and covered him. He told him that he was going after someone to help take him home. As Chief He Dog came out of the building, he saw the army officer, White Hat, and his interpreter, Blaila, across the grounds. He walked up to them and asked them if they knew what happened. They said that they were trying to find out.

Chief He Dog, said, "You promised in a treaty that we both swore to, that nothing like this would happen again; that there would be no more blood shed." With these words, he slapped the officer, White Hat, across the face.

There was a bridge across the White River, leading to the fort. Soldiers were patrolling the bridge that evening. White Hat told Chief He Dog through his interpreter, Blaila, to stay at the fort overnight. But He Dog left. As he went across this bridge, he came upon Chief Crazy Horse's mother, father, and a close relative, named Against the Sky (Touch the Clouds) coming toward the fort. Crazy Horse's father asked He

Dog how his friend was, so He Dog said, "They stabbed him but he is not dead yet. But you must hurry to him." With these words, he went past them.

It is not known who took Chief Crazy Horse to the hospital at the fort. It is believed that someone on duty did. The preacher from the church stayed with him all night until he died.

Before he died, it is said that he raised an arm toward the sky and seemed to be trying to say something. Only his lips were moving. Perhaps he was praying to the Great Spirit.

After Chief Crazy Horse passed away to the Happy Hunting grounds, his people came after him at the fort hospital. His father, mother, and his wife put him on a travois hitched to a horse and started back to their camp. When they came to the camp, Chief Crazy Horse's folks held a sort of funeral service for him. All the Indian tribes had come together there. After this, Chief Crazy Horse's folks took their dead son with them to Chief Spotted Tail's camp. Later, a small frame house was built by the soldiers, in which Chief Crazy Horse's body was placed and guarded.

These Indians were to be taken to reservations by groups or tribes. The tribe known as the Rosebud Sioux were to be taken along the Missouri River. This tribe left one day and Chief Crazy Horse's folks left with them, taking their dead son's body along. The Oglala Sioux left for Holy Butte, somewhere else along the Missouri River.

Chief Crazy Horse was thirty-two years old when he was killed. His close friend, Chief He Dog, was thirty-three years old at the time. This was in September, in the year of 1877. Chief Crazy Horse was killed at Fort Robinson in the state of Nebraska. He died by a soldier's bayonet.

# The Killing of Chief Crazy Horse

Chief Crazy Horse had several names during his lifetime. When he was a baby, he was named Light Hair, because he had very light-colored hair. Later, when he was a boy, he was called Buys-A-Bad-Woman, Crushes-Man, or a Horse-Partly-Showing. His father was an Oglala Sioux. His mother was a Minikowoju Sioux. He was not a very big man. He was of medium stature and build.

He acquired the name Crazy Horse in a fight with another tribe. During the fight, he rammed his horse into the enemies' horses, knocking the riders off. He did this repeatedly. After the fight he was given the name, Crazy Horse.

The men listed below grew up with Chief Crazy Horse. They played with him as a boy. Later they fought in wars with him, and knew him well.

Chief He Dog          Chief Short Bull
Chief Pretty Weasel   Chief Loneman

This history was told to me by my father, Chief He Dog, and some of the others mentioned above. At the time Chief Crazy Horse was killed, I was eight years old.

It is to be assumed that Chief Crazy Horse was killed because of what he was and what he did as a Chief, a protector and provider for his tribe. It was perhaps also due to the resentment and jealousy on the part of the chiefs and headmen of the other tribes. It was the cowardly way in which he was killed that anyone would object to.

Up to the present time, no one knows where Chief Crazy Horse was buried. It has been said that he was buried at Wounded Knee, Porcupine, White Clay, Eagle Nest Butte, and other places. It can't be proved that he was buried at any of the places mentioned.

# Obituary of Five Oglala Sioux Chiefs

All of these men were made chiefs at the same time when they were young men.

1. CARRIES SWORD
   This chief met death from natural causes at Fort Robinson in the state of Nebraska. He was [first ?] of these five to pass away to the happy Hunting grounds.

2. CHIEF CRAZY HORSE
   This chief, the most famous of the five, also met death at Fort Robinson in the state of Nebraska at the hands of a United States soldier's bayonet.

3. CHIEF YOUNG MAN AFRAID OF HIS HORSES
   This chief met death of natural causes while visiting in Crow Agency in the state of Montana.

4. CHIEF AMERICAN HORSE
   This chief met death of natural causes at his home in Kyle on the Pine Ridge Indian Reservation.

5. CHIEF HE DOG
   This chief was the last to pass away from natural causes at his son's home on the Pine Ridge Reservation at the age of one hundred years and four months.

The history of Chief Crazy Horse and the obituaries of the five Oglala Sioux chiefs [who] were related to the Rev. Joseph Eagle Hawk. Rev. Eagle Hawk was also a judge for a number of years at the Pine Ridge Indian Agency.

# William Garnett's Account

# Introductory Note

For some years now historians and students have shown a growing appreciation for the Garnett interviews and narratives. One of the latest to do so is Dr. James Olson who made considerable use of the interviews in his *Red Cloud and the Sioux Problem* (see Bibliography for complete citation).

William Garnett was the only child of Major Richard Garnett, Commandant at Fort Laramie; his mother was Sioux. Richard Garnett was a member of a very old, very distinguished Maryland family, and a graduate of the United States Military Academy where they still have an oil portrait of him. When the Civil War broke out Major Garnett offered his services to the Confederacy, became a general, and was killed in Pickett's charge at Gettysburg. William stayed on with his mother's people and, when grown, served the United States Army officers as scout and interpreter, especially during the hectic days of the later 1870s. Born in 1855, he was 22 years old at the time of the Crazy Horse killing.

He was an intelligent man, quite at home in either the red or the white world. In his capacity as interpreter, he was in on all events and privy to the most private happenings. He knew almost everyone in the Fort Robinson region, either red or white; he was a shrewd observer with a marvelous memory and practically total recall. As an eye witness and participant in these various happenings his narrative is priceless.

The man directly responsible for this practically unknown narrative was General Hugh Scott. From his first assignment to the Seventh Cavalry in 1876, during his long and honorable army service, and through his final duty as Chief of Staff, Scott was interested in the Indian. He studied Indians all his life, becoming familiar with their customs and dialects, and often acting as official interpreter during conferences. He became the Army's leading expert on the Indian sign language in which he was so adept that he offered a reward for any sign he could not read. He told of the differences among Indians in using the sign language, most of them making their signs in a circle of 24 to 30 inches in diameter, but he really had to concentrate with Red Cloud who made his signs in the usual manner but within a circle of no more than 12 inches.

In his search for the truth in history, General Scott visited Pine Ridge in 1920, and asked William Garnett to relate the Crazy Horse story. Present also was Major McLaughlin, the Indian agent, plus a stenographer to make a word for word record, a copy of which was given to Garnett.

The following account was copied directly from Garnett's personal transcript, which is before me as this is being written.

CARROLL FRISWOLD

# William Garnett's Account

*General H. L. Scott and Major James McLaugh-
lin ask of William Garnett, aged sixty-five, interpreter at Pine Ridge, South Dakota, to tell them
the story of the death of Crazy Horse, a noted chief
of the Northern Oglala Sioux, at Fort Robinson,
Nebraska, in the month of September, 1877.*

Red Cloud went out after Crazy Horse, and couriers
came in with Red Cloud and they wanted supplies, that
is, grub, and I went out with Lieutenant Rosencrans
with some wagons loaded with rations and some beef
cattle. A scout was driving the cattle. We met him on
Sage Creek, and turned the beef and rations over to
Crazy Horse's band, and moved in with him and we
returned to the Agency in about three days. A little
before we got to the Agency, Lieutenant Clark, acting
as General Crook's staff, came out to meet Crazy Horse,
about four miles northwest of the Agency. He shook
hands with Crazy Horse and other Northern chiefs out
there on the prairie, and the Northern Indians dressed
up Lieutenant Clark, an army officer, with Indian
dress, a war shirt, war bonnet and pipe. They shook
hands with the left hand because the heart is on the left
side. Some old fellow said, "Shake hands with him
with your left hand for that is the side your heart lays."
Clark told Crazy Horse as soon as they put him in
the camp, "You want to take up all the guns and
ponies." The horses they were going to turn over to the
Indian scouts, and the scouts could do just as they

wanted to with the horses. So then we went through the lodges taking up the guns, and the horses were taken and turned over to the Indian scouts. We had scouts there, Cheyennes, Arapahoes, and Sioux, but the Sioux were doing this work. So that was all that was done at that time.

Next, they were turned over to the Indian Agent [James Irwin-ed.], and he took them up and gave them rations, and something like about a couple of weeks after they came in, Lieutenant Clark, (the Indians called him "White Hat") he said he was going to make Crazy Horse a scout, and nineteen others. This man Clark was going to do this. I went out to the Crazy Horse village and told Crazy Horse that Lieutenant Clark would make him a scout and nineteen of his Indians, so when I told him that, they jumped at the chance. They came and got arms and pistols. So Crazy Horse was a scout. He started in in about the same month, about May. So we got along with Crazy Horse pretty good, just the same as any friendly Indian for some time, and in the month of August got the news that the Nez Percé had broken out and were working toward Wyoming. Clark was going to take some scouts out there where this Nez Percé trouble was, and we had Crazy Horse and other Indians consult over trying to go out and take these Nez Percé Indians. Crazy Horse said if he was going, he was going to take all his lodges and he was going to hunt at the same time. Clark said that he didn't want the lodges and women; that he just wanted the men.

In two or three days General Crook and the General of the Platte Department, they arrived and told all of the Indians that they would hold a council on White Clay. So this council was arranged and General Crook was going to be there. I stayed with Baptiste Pourier, but he went ahead of General Crook and me to the Agency. While we were at the Agency ahead of them, an Indian scout named Woman Dress came up to us and said, "Where are you going?" We told him that we were going to White Clay to an Indian council with General Crook and Lieutenant Clark and we were waiting for them. He said, "Don't you go there with General Crook. When you hold this council at White Clay, Crazy Horse is going to come in there with sixty Indians, and catch General Crook by the hand, like he is going to shake hands, and he is going to hold on to him, and those sixty Indians are going to kill Crook and whoever he has with him."

Just about then, General Crook came up with an ambulance, which would hold nine men. It was a fancy one. Well they came up and started for this White Clay. Lieutenant Clark knew the place. Baptiste Pourier ran ahead of the team and stopped him and he said, "Now tell Crook what this Indian said." This Woman Dress, he was right there. So the team was stopped, and I told General Crook just what this man, Woman Dress, said. I said, "General, this man says there is a man by the name of Little Wolf, an Indian scout, who told his brother Lone Bear (he died a couple years ago) that they were going to kill General Crook at that council just as he said here, and Woman Dress said they were going to kill him." Then General Crook studied a little bit, and he asked me, "What do you know about this man, Woman Dress? Is he reliable? Does he tell the truth?" And I said, "General, this is a big undertaking and I could not say – I am going to leave it up to Baptiste Pourier, a man who is with me, and he will tell you. This is how close they are related – Baptiste's wife's mother and Woman Dress' wife's mother were sisters, so their wives are first cousins." So I turned that part over to Pourier, about what he would say about Woman Dress, and Bat says, "General, I want to tell you this man is a truthful man and whatever he tells you is the truth." So Crook studied again and said, "I never start any place but what I like to get there." Lieutenant Clark said, "General, it is no use to go." He said, "I am not anybody, or these men – we have lost a man just like you, when we lost General Custer. We miss him, and we couldn't replace any man in his place alive. There is no use for you to start in there when you have no protection, just like that other was." General Crook [said] "What excuse I can make I do not know." Lieutenant Clark says, "You leave that to me." And General Crook said, "Alright." Then Lieutenant Clark says to me, "Billy, you go to the council and tell them that a message has come for General Crook and he had to go back." He gave me a lot of Indian names – some eight names and he names them over to me, and he told me to tell those men to report to Fort Robinson right away. So I went on to this council at White Clay that General Crook was going to hold, and the council was on. There was a lot of Indians there when I got to this place. When I arrived, Crazy Horse was not there and none of his followers were there either. I did not see any of them in this council. So I got American Horse, and I told him just exactly what I was told to tell in that council, and when I told him, he says this, "Leave that up to me – I am going to tell why he went back." He picked out the different names I had and said, "I will attend to that." I watched American Horse's move. He went in the council lodge and he said, "General Crook was coming, but he got a letter on the way and he had

to go back there, and that is why he isn't here, the interpreter just tells me. So he won't be here today." I saw
the old fellow sneak around to these Indians and he
whispered to them. And so when he did that, he came
up and said, "You go home – I will bring those men
up." So I went back to Fort Robinson and I told General Crook and Lieutenant Clark that the Indians were
coming – those that they wanted – and they came there
in about one-half hour after I got there. They plotted
how to get ahold of this man, Crazy Horse. It was told
there about his trying to do away with Crook. Those
friendly Indians were surprised to hear that they were
going to get away with Crook as they didn't know anything about it. So it was planned that every one of those
Indian chiefs was going to pick out four brave men of
their respective bands, and that night those picked men
were going to the Crazy Horse village (Crazy Horse's
people did not mix with the others; they had a separate
village of their own) and kill Crazy Horse. The man
who actually killed him was going to get $300.00. There
was a horse Lieutenant Clark had, and he was also
going to get that horse. Now this was a kind of private
council in General Bradley's apartments, but he was
not there, he was at his office. Those present were General Crook, Lieutenant Clark, Frank Gruard, Baptiste
Pourier and myself, and the rest were all Indians, Red
Cloud, Little Wound, Red Dog, Young Man Afraid of
His Horse, No Flesh, Yellow Bear, High Wolf, Slow
Bull, Black Bear, American Horse, Three Bears, Blue
Horse and No Water. These are all Oglalas. So they
said they were going to draw some ammunition, and
they did and took it with them, which was late in the
afternoon then. I was there and was told to stay close
around the post. While I was around the post, there

was an orderly came up for me, and he says, "Garnett, you are wanted at General Bradley's quarters and you are to take the back way and go into the house." So when I went and went in to Bradley's room, this was Bradley's sitting room, where we had this council, same place – the Indian Agent was there, Interpreter Leon Pallidy, an Indian by the name of He Dog, a Northern Indian and General Bradley. When I got in the room, Bradley says, "What was that council that was held here today in my room?" He asked me in the presence of this Northern chief, He Dog, and I was afraid to answer because he was on the opposite side, and I said, "General, isn't there some other room where you and I can go?" So he took me to about a third room away from those men. So when I went all alone with him, about the third room, I asked him why he had asked me those questions before a Northern Indian, and Bradley tells me, "Was it not planned out in my room there for these Indians to kill Crazy Horse; the man who kills Crazy Horse to get $300.00 and Lieutenant Clark's running horse – that is what the Agent and those Indians had come up there for?" I said, "Is there any catch about this? Where did you get it?" He said, "These three men came up here with this story." I says, "General, that was supposed to be a private council and not to be given out, and I see you have a Northern Indian in there and I did not want to talk to you in his presence." I told him the plan was made, and about this $300.00 and horse racket; that ammunition was drawn and the Indians were to be prepared for it. He says, "You go back where the orderly found you, and stay there." So I went back to the sutler's, and I was there probably one-half hour, when the next soldier came for me. It was Lieutenant Clark's orderly. He says, "Garnett, Clark wants you." So I went to Lieutenant Clark's quarters and went in the room, and he was walking up and down in there. When I went in he said, "These Indians can hold nothing." He says, "Bradley has got hold of that council we had with the Indians today, so you go down to the Indian village right away, and stop them Indians from approaching Crazy Horse. When you go down, tell those Indians not to disturb Crazy Horse, but tell all to report to Fort Robinson before sun-up in the morning." So I went down to the place called White Clay, where I went before, where that council was going to take place before, and I got to American Horse's lodge and I met a bunch of Indians back of his lodge plotting up something when I got there. I told them not to bother themselves; not to kill Crazy Horse that night; that this was the message that Lieutenant Clark gave me, but to report to Fort Robinson before sun-up and draw ammunition and guns.

This was the next morning, and the Indians all arrived. Those that had no guns, drew guns. So guns and ammunition were drawn to start to the Crazy Horse village. So we got started out. Crazy Horse was down White River about six miles northeast of Fort Robinson, so there were soldiers, Indian scouts, and also all of the friendly Indians were with us and went down to the Crazy Horse village. Some of them was on the west side of the creek and some was on the east side of the creek (there were two parties). Just a little before we got into the Crazy Horse village, the messenger says, "Crazy Horse is either going to fight or he is going to run away; he is catching his horse." So I was with one gang. I was on the east side of the creek and Lieutenant Clark was on the west side. One of the scouts tells me, "You go and see Clark. If them Indians attempt to fight, we are going to do it too." I left the gang I was with and went over to see Clark. I told the Indian, "Take it easy, and I will run over and see Clark." I met an Indian on the way, Looking Horse of the Cheyenne Agency. He was a scout and he had one of our guns. He says, "Where are you going? I have just scolded Clark and I am coming to scold the crowd you are with." So, when I got to Lieutenant Clark I said, "It looks like they are going to sure fight, and if they do, we are going to fight back." He says, "Go ahead, but don't shoot unless they start in on you. I sent Looking Horse down to join the rest of the scouts. Did you meet him?" I said, "He said that he scolded you. He was sassy when I met him."

I returned to my former command, and on the way going back, I saw a big black object behind me about one-quarter of a mile or so. It was something large and black and was still, and there was something small moving along the ledge on the road. When I got back, I was told this Looking Horse that I had met, had his horse shot from under him and he was pounded up. That was the black object I had seen behind. That was done while I was off to see Clark. Woman Dress killed the horse, and two or three of them pounded up the man and they took his gun and pistol. He was friendly to the Crazy Horse party.

We got near the mouth of the Little White Clay and we saw a lot of horsemen there and we halted. They were Crazy Horse's war-men and were all dressed up in war clothes. Little Big Man comes over to us where we halted and he said, "It looks like Crazy Horse is going to show a fight," and those men right off the hill ran down, all of them, and ahead of them was a young man not older than sixteen years, he was a large boy.

He was in the Custer fight when he was only fifteen. He held a six-shooter in his hand and he was ahead of these other Indians and he came right to us. He was right in the lead and we all halted and when he came in, we gave him room, but he did not shoot. Just then, another fellow came up. He was on a pinto horse, and that man had a war-bonnet on, all worked out behind with about one hundred feathers – a double bonnet – he came up. He did not say that he was a chief. They never presented this man before, but on that day, he was the biggest chief there. His name was Black Fox. He came up and he said this, "Men, ever since I have been big enough to fight, I have been looking for one. I never was killed up to this time – and I have seen nothing but the clouds and the ground." That is the time that he pulled his knife out and put it in his mouth. He had a Springfield carbine and a six-shooter, and American Horse said, "Brother-in-law, hold on, let up, save the women and children," and he handed him a pipe, pointing the stem of the pipe at him. He said, "Hold on, we have not come down for anything like that; we came down to save you. Don't you make any trouble." Then he said to the others, "Look out, cock your guns, be ready, and see whether he smokes this pipe. Don't do anything, but see whether he smoked this pipe." Black Fox said, "How," and jumped up and shook hands with American Horse and they sat down together, and I noticed this double bonnet. They faced the others and smoked together. We were, about twenty-five of us, in line, about fifteen feet behind American Horse when he smoked. The man spoke this way, "Crazy Horse has gone with his wife, stampede to Rosebud, so I have got the village, and I thought I would die for them, but I am glad to hear you are peaceable." and he said that Crazy Horse had gone to Camp Sheridan, and he thought he had to stand for the village, and he thought he had to die today. He said, "If this is all, I am glad to hear it." While these two men smoked, those Indians were running back and forth before us, but they did not shoot. They were ready to protect these men. There were about 30 of them. Finally, this man says, "Hey, stop this running and get back there." They were all ready to stampede, and the minute that he announced that word, they all disappeared and showed no fight. That very man had the control of that village.

Lieutenant Clark came up to where we were and said that somebody had alarmed Crazy Horse, and he was gone with some 28 or 30 men to follow him. Clark said, "Pick out twelve men from this gang, too, and No Water would be in charge of the twelve men and they would have to follow up Crazy Horse," and then we went back to bring them into the Agency, the friendly Indians and the others too and put them all together in front of the Agency, all the Sioux and the Cheyennes. This was along about August that this was going on. So we got back home, and the next day, some of the scouts got back late, something like four o'clock – those that followed him up – and they said that Crazy Horse was coming back to Fort Robinson the next day with Lee. It was about three o'clock when they arrived at Fort Robinson, and Clark sends me down there and tells me to tell the officer to put Crazy Horse in the guard house, so I went down and I got within something like 35 or 40 feet from the door of the adjutant's office, when they came out from the adjutant's office and the officer of the day and Little Big Man, they had Crazy Horse, and he was walking in the middle. There

TOUCH THE CLOUDS, A CHIEF OF THE MINNECONJU
Occasionally identified as an uncle of Crazy Horse — a
brother of the mother of Crazy Horse. He was a very
large man, seven feet tall, hence his name; he was also
known as Against the Sky. He stayed in the adjutant's
office with Crazy Horse until the wounded Chief died.
Courtesy of Nebraska State Historical Society.

WILLIAM GARNETT, 1855-1929, AND HIS FAMILY

BAPTISTE "BIG BAT" POURIER AND WILLIAM GARNETT

A remarkable photograph, found by Fred Hackett at
Pine Ridge Reservation, showing the young Garnett with
Pourier. The only other photo of Big Bat with which I am
familiar is in the Denver Public Library Western Collection, showing a considerably older man with a full beard.
Shortly after the above photo was made, Big Bat went
on a fire-water party with some of his Indian friends.
During the affair things got out of hand, a fight ensued
and Big Bat was badly beaten and his jaw was broken.
Due to rather crude medical care in the Indian country,
it is possible that his jaw was a bit crooked after it healed,
and he may have grown the beard to hide the deformity.

CHIEF LITTLE BIG MAN

Garnett describes him as a loyal friend of Crazy Horse.
Marie Sandoz saw him as a villain and traitor.
Bourke attributes to him considerable ability and force.
Whether his purpose was good or bad, when Crazy Horse was
stabbed, Little Big Man was holding the Chief, trying to
prevent him from fighting. Thus was fulfilled the prophecy,
given to Crazy Horse as a young man, that he would be killed
while his arms were being held by one of his own people.

**WOMAN'S DRESS**
Jealous of Crazy Horse, he lied when he reported to the
authorities that Crazy Horse was plotting
to kill General Crook.
Courtesy of Nebraska State Historical Society.

was quite a number of other Indians and they were
walking right for the guard house, about 60 yards away.
So I was walking back and watching and that crowd
was walking for the guard house, and I went back and
went along almost straight west from the guard house,
and I had to go northwest of this to get back to Lieutenant Clarks, and finally, I saw them go into the guard
house. I was watching because I was told to put him in
the guard house, and I saw them go into the guard house
with him. After they all went in, it was probably one-
half a minute, something happened in there. I could
hear the noise inside. There was confusion going on and
I stopped. There was a sentinel walking up and down
between the cannon and the guard house. There was a
lot of cannon in front of the guard house. I stopped and
looked, and I must have been something like, probably
60 or 70 feet from that guard house door, and I saw a
Roman-nosed Indian come out. He had a very thin
face. He was a Rosebud Indian. He says, "This is a
guard house." A lot of horsemen, a lot of Indians were
outside. They were Crazy Horse's people. There were
Rosebud Indians, Cheyennes, Arapahoes, and some of
our own people. The Arapahoes took part with these
friendly Indians all the time. So when Crazy Horse ran
out, there was a lot of other people following him.
There was a storm door. I saw Indians and guards in
there and they were running out. The prisoners with
shackles on them; that is, deserters, white prisoners,
with balls and chains on them, they were all coming out
through the door and those iron balls were what made
all the noise. Among them, I saw Crazy Horse and
Little Big Man coming out. Little Big Man had Crazy
Horse by the wrists, and Crazy Horse had a knife in
one of his hands and he was trying to break loose from

## The Killing of Chief Crazy Horse

Little Big Man, and he said, "Let me go, let me go; you won't allow me to hurt anyone!" And Little Big Man said, . . .* Little Big Man in the pit of his stomach with the butt end of his gun and knocked him backward on the ground. As he struck Little Big Man, he said, "You have done this once before." So he struck him and he was sitting down there and supporting himself with both arms. The friendly Indians of whom Swift Bear was one, they said to Crazy Horse, "We told you to behave yourself." When the sentinel stabbed him, Crazy Horse said, "He has killed me now!" When Swift Bear caught him, Yankton Charlie was standing behind him and drew out Crazy Horse's revolver from the scabbard, and in about a minute they let him go and he sat right down there and was falling over and I left to go over to Lieutenant Clarks. All these Indians separated; the Crazy Horse Indians going toward General

---

* At this most critical point, unfortunately, a section of the manuscript is missing. C.F. (The publisher wishes to note that this account was also published in an abbreviated and reworded form in Byrne, *Soldiers of the Plains*. The following excerpt from that account appears to be much condensed. We will pick it up just prior to the missing section, and follow it until there is a duplication with the original presented above. "Little Big Man had Crazy Horse by the wrists and Crazy Horse had a knife in one of his hands and he was trying to break loose from Little Big Man. Just then, when they came out of the door, the sentinel had his bayonet at Crazy Horse and made a little pass, just enough to touch him. I always thought that the sentinel did not intend to stab Crazy Horse, but only to touch him so that he would drop his knife. But in the struggle, Crazy Horse stumbled against the bayonet.

"It did not appear to me that Crazy Horse was stabbed as badly as he was. Doctor McGillycuddy, the surgeon, after examination, said that the bayonet went through both kidneys and within one-half inch of going through his body.

"When the sentinel stabbed him, Crazy Horse said, 'He has killed me now.' "

Bradley's quarters, which was on the east end of the officers line. The friendly Indians went over to Lieutenant Clark's which was on the west end of the line. When I got there, Clark says, "What is the matter with Crazy Horse?" I said, "He is stabbed!" He said, "Take him and put him in the Adjutant's office," and he said, "You can go with him." So we went back again and American Horse said, "I don't know how badly Crazy Horse is hurt," and he said to put him in a blanket and take him into the Adjutant's office, which they did. Red Shirt and Two Dogs helped to carry Crazy Horse into the office. After he was put in, Chief American Horse said, "We have been wrangling over this Crazy Horse; we have got him in the house now and you can't touch him."

Crazy Horse was stabbed in the left side and died at 11 o'clock that night. Dr. McGillycuddy was with him when he died. Soon his father came up after he was put in the office, about sundown. He wanted to go in, and he had on his quiver, and I says, "Old man, you cannot get in there unless you give up your knife," but he gave up his bows, arrows and his knife. The father's name also was Crazy Horse. He gave up his arms and went in to see his son. Touch The Cloud and another Northern Indian was taking care of him. Louis Bordeaux came up with Lee from Sheridan with Crazy Horse. We went to bed in Clark's quarters, all three in one bed. Frank Gruard was on the other side of the room. We slept underneath a window. I had two six-shooters under my head, and Bordeaux had two and Bat had two. I was awakened in the night by somebody pulling my hair. It was Crazy Horse's father looking in the window and telling me to wake up. He said, "My son is dead and I want my bow and arrows." I turned and looked up at him and saw who it was and told him to

95

hold up – that I would get fixed up. Then I slipped my revolvers away so he could not snatch them and I waked up Bordeaux and told him that the man was dead and to hide his six-shooters; then we waked up Bat Pourier, and we all got our six-shooters. Frank Gruard was on the other side of the room laughing at us, and Bat Pourier said, "How did you know that old man, Crazy Horse, was there?" He said, "I saw him before he waked up Garnett." Bat was very angry and he said, "Everytime we are up against anything dangerous, you are always out of the way; you are a coward! He might have taken up one of those revolvers and shot Billy or Bordeaux." I told the old man that he couldn't get his bow and arrows. I could do nothing; that would have to be the order of a commanding officer; that I dare not go to him at night. I told him that he would just have to cry it out about his son, but I couldn't get him his bow and arrows. Lieutenant Clark slept in the next room. He told us beforehand that if anything happened to come and wake him. So the four of us went in. I said, "Clark, wake up!" He was sound asleep. I said, "Fellows, let us take him out of the bed," and we had him by the legs and swung him. It looked to me as if he had taken something to put him to sleep. I said, "Clark, Crazy Horse is dead." Clark says, "You go to bed; you are all played out. You are all afraid of him." So I said that the soldiers were all afraid of him. So he went back to bed and so did we.

Nine or ten years afterwards I found out that what Woman Dress said about attempting to kill General Crook was not true. This was all framed up against him; not by white people, but by Indians who were jealous of him. About nine or ten years later, I was in the guard house here and Little Wolf and Lone Bear were policemen. Little Wolf was sitting in the guard house one night with me and he said, "Now we came in from the north with Crazy Horse; we intended to be peaceable with the white people – the same as the other Indians. I wonder why Crazy Horse was treated the way he was and finally died." And I thought back and I said, "You killed him." And he said, "I killed him?" And I said, "Yes, you killed him." And he said, "I killed Crazy Horse when I came in from the North with him and was a scout with him? Come, how did I kill him?" I told him that his talk had killed him. I said, "You told your own brother, Lone Bear, that Crazy Horse was going to kill General Crook." He said, "I never told my brother I heard Crazy Horse say it." [The editor has found that Mr. Friswold's manuscript is lacking another section of material which appeared, possibly in abbreviated form, in Byrne, *Soldiers of the Plains.* The following text in italic type is taken from that work. We begin and end with the line which duplicates Mr. Friswold's text.] *He replied, "I never told my brother any such stuff. I never knew that I had anything to do with this. I am going to see my brother." So the next time I met him he came to me with Lone Bear, his brother, and he denied that he told Woman Dress that General Crook was going to be killed. "I never told Woman Dress any such thing," he said.*

*About three months afterwards, they caught Woman Dress near Fort Robinson, and Woman Dress came up to me with Louis Shangreau (his nephew) and said, "You can tell as good a lie as any one I ever saw." I said, "Woman Dress, what am I lying about?" And he said, "You lied about me. I heard Crazy Horse say, 'To-morrow there is going to be a council on over at White Clay, the Indian village, and Crook's going to be there. I will catch Crook by the hand and pretend*

*like I was going to shake hands with him and make
quick work of him and whoever he will have with him.'
Now that is what I heard Crazy Horse say. You said in
the guard house* [We resume with the Friswold manuscript at this point. Ed.] that Little Wolf was the one
who told Lone Bear and Lone Bear told me. It was me,
myself, that heard Crazy Horse, and now you tell lies
about me and saying that I got it from this Lone Bear."

Just about the time I got this roasting and I was facing these two men, Louis Shangreau and Woman Dress,
I felt something touch me behind and it was Baptiste
Pourier. I turned around and shook hands with Bat and
said, "You came here just in time." I told Louis Shangreau that Bat knew all about this and he will finish it
with you. I told them that I was not afraid of them.
I told him that he and his uncle were not telling the
truth, and Bat explained this whole trouble about what
took place back in 1877 when Crazy Horse was killed.
Bat said, "I will tell – I know just exactly how it happened." He told just how it occurred and Louis Shangreau was mad at his uncle then and turned around and
said, "You are a big liar and you are the cause of a
good man's death and you are jealous of him." Then
Bat, with his finger pointed at Woman Dress, told him,
"You are a liar and you are the cause of a good man's
death." And Louis Shangreau said the same thing and
Woman Dress never said a word.

He is now all broken up and lives on Wounded Knee
and draws a pension. I was a witness in his pension case.
I told the officer that I ought not to be a witness in his
pension case, but he was a scout and he had been
wounded and I was a witness for him. He got $240.00
back pay and $40.00 per month.

I told General Crook about this when he came here
in 1889. Bat and I were together and told him. "Bat,"

General Crook said, "Billy knew more than you did, he did not recommend Woman Dress that time. I ought to have gone to that council and I should not have listened to Clark. I never started any place but I got there."

The way this came up, Crook was here at a council in 1889 when they were dividing up this Reservation. Woman Dress reported that Little Hawk wanted to make some trouble about signing the Treaty, and he was talking very sassy. General Crook sent for Little Hawk and said, "Why are you making trouble about this Treaty?" Little Hawk told General Crook, "I dressed up Lieutenant Clark with a war bonnet when we first surrendered, and dressed up McGillycuddy when I first came back from Canada," and he said, "I have been faithful to you people; now you killed Crazy Horse; now are you going to kill me? Your Indians are telling lies about me like they told about Crazy Horse and now are you going to kill me?" Crook said, "No, I found out about what made the trouble about Crazy Horse afterward; you Indians made the trouble – I felt sorry for that." Little Hawk was told that he could sign or leave it alone. He said, "I am afraid of it – we sign for certain things, and after you people go away, you get other things down in the treaty that were not there. I find in all of these Treaties it is the same way. I am afraid of that; I am afraid to touch that pen." Crook told him, "Alright, it is up to you; it is better for you to sign, but you can sign or not just as you wish." He told General Crook that he was going to see McGillycuddy up at Rapid City, and if he says it is alright, I will sign it. He went up to Rapid City to see McGillycuddy, and when he came back, he signed it.

It is a great pity that Crazy Horse was killed for he had the reputation of being one of the bravest men that ever lived. All the fights in Wyoming, the soldiers were all firing at Crazy Horse and trying to kill him. There are a great many old soldiers at Hot Springs, South Dakota, now, who could tell you about shooting at Crazy Horse. Crazy Horse was no politician about talking, but he was one of the bravest men among the Sioux. The Crow Indians used to say, "We know Crazy Horse better than we do you other Sioux. Whenever we have a fight, he is closer to us than he is to you." The way they recognized him in a fight was that he always wore a colt hide as a cape.

# The Correspondence of McGillyucddy and Garnett

# Introductory Note

The following correspondence by and between William Garnett and Dr. Valentine McGillycuddy was written in the 1920s when the doctor was house physician at the Claremont Hotel in Berkeley, California. It deals primarily with the historical events of the 1870s in which both men were involved. The most important item, of course, is that in which McGillycuddy describes the events of September 5, 1877. Unfortunately several of the answering letters written by Garnett have not turned up, but there is still interesting and important information to be gleaned from the available ones which appear here.

One of them contains the answer to a question which has long puzzled students – why did Crazy Horse call off the Rosebud fight when he had a very good chance to destroy Crook's force? The answer is quite logical: the Indians had ridden twenty miles to get into position to surprise Crook, they had given him enough of a trouncing so that he went into camp to wait for reinforcements, then they simply quit the fight to get some food and rest. If you notice, Crazy Horse had planned far ahead when he ordered the camps to move toward the fighting, so his men would be that much closer to food and rest at the end of the day. Another interesting comment of the doctor's was that Crazy Horse was a good man and he would trust him anywhere. Each letter has been copied exactly, even to the spelling and punctuation.

CARROLL FRISWOLD

Dr. Valentine T. McGillycuddy, 1849-1939

# The Correspondence of Dr. Valentine McGillycuddy and William Garnett

Pine Ridge, So. Dak.
June 20, 1921.

Mr. Malcolm McDowell,
Washington, D.C.

Dear Mr. McDowell: In reply to your letter of June 15, 1921, I will give you the list, as well as I can of the Guides, Scouts, Interpreters and packers that were with the outfit that I was with during the campaign of 1876.

*Guide*

| Frank Gruard | | Died about 1908 |
|---|---|---|

*Interpreters*

| William Garnett | | Sioux Interpreter |
|---|---|---|
| Pine Ridge, S.D. | | |
| William Rowland | | Cheyenne Interpreter |
| Died about 1905 | | |

*Chief Scouts*

| Baptiste Pourier | Sioux Scout | Manderson, S.D. |
|---|---|---|
| Louie Richard | " | Died about 1897 |
| Louis Shangreau | " | Died about 1899 |
| Luke North | Pawnee Scout | Omaha, Nebr. |
| | | when last heard of |
| Frank North | " | Died years ago (1885) |
| Bill Crosby | Shoshone Scout | Ft. Washakee, Wyo. (Think he is dead) |

As far as I know Baptiste Pourier and myself are all of this outfit that are living. They were all older men than myself so they must be dead by this time as I am 66 years old now.

I want to thank you very much for your interest in this matter and assure you I appreciate your efforts very much. This pension, if it passes will be a great help to me as I am unable to make enough to properly support myself and family.

Respectfully,    [WM. GARNETT]

------

HOTEL CLAREMONT
Berkeley, California.

February 28, 1922.

Wm. Garnett,

Dear Sir: I wonder if you are still alive or have "gone over the range."

I am getting along in years myself, had my 73d birthday on the 14th, but am still active and in good health.

If you receive this will you give me information on the following.

Was not Young-Man-Afraid killed by a fall from his horse in the spring of 1901 following the Wounded Knee fight, and how old was he.

What relation was American Horse No. 2, killed at Slim Buttes in September 1876, to our American Horse.

How did Crazy Horse get his name, was his father's name Crazy Horse, and was he a chief by birth, was he an Uncpapa and his wife an Oglala.

About Little Wound, what relative of his did Red Cloud kill and how and when, how long has Little Wound been dead and how old was he.

What battle did he lead the Indians in and won out,

was it not Ash Hollow, Nebraska, who commanded the troops and about what year was it.

About when did Old-Man-Afraid die, and how old was he, how did he get his name.

What was Little Wound's fathers name.

I hope I have not asked you too many questions.

I shall be glad to hear from you and hope that you are having good health.

When did Sword die.

Your friend,     V. T. MᴄGɪʟʟʏᴄᴜᴅᴅʏ

---

Pine Ridge, So. Dak.
March 6, 1922.

Mr. V. T. McGillicuddy.
Hotel Clairmont, Berkley, Cal.

My Dear Friend: I received your letter of February 28, 1922, asking information regarding several old Indians of this reservation last Saturday but I delayed answering until today for I wanted to make sure of some of the dates.

Young Man Afraid was on his way to visit the Crow Indians of Montana and died of heart failure on the road, some place between Edgemont, So. Dak. and Newcastle, Wyo. in 1894.

In the fight at Slim Butte in 1876 there were two Indians killed, an old man whose name I do not know and a young man names Iron Shield. Bat Pourier killed him. Neither of these men were named American Horse and were no relation to our American Horse, the chief.

Crazy Horse is all Sioux but his father was an Oglala, and his mother was a Minni-ko-wo-jun (Cheyenne River Agency, So. Dak.) He took his name from his father who was also named Crazy Horse. He was not a chief by birth but was chosen chief in 1868, on account of his fighting ability. There is no question but that he was the bravest and best fighter in the Sioux nation.

There were four Sioux and one Cheyenne killed in the Rosebud fight and a few more wounded that recovered. This is what Red Feather, a brother in law of Crazy Horse says.

The creek on which the Custer fight was held is called Greezy Grass by the Indians, and Little Big Horn by the Crows and white people.

After the fight the Indians struck south east for a little while. The Cheyenne Indians separated from the Sioux and went South into the Wolf Mountains, crossing them and going on the west side. The Oglala Sioux stayed in the Big Horn Mountains. The Sitting Bull Indians went North, crossed the Yellowstone, where they had a little fight with General Miles and then went on to Canada. The Minnekoju Indians left Sitting Bull and did not go to Canada with him, but crossed the Yellowstone and came south. The reason the Indians split up was that they were running short of food and had to split up so they could get game, for so large a bunch could not be provided for.

I hope this is the information you want. Of course Red Feather would not exaggerate the number of Indians killed in the Rosebud fight, for he was one of the fighting men.

Frank Goings told me he has received several letters from you. Don't go too much on Frank tells you. He is married to a daughter of Old John Nelson, and if John were now living, Frank would give him a close run for being the champion liar of the world.

Yours very truly,    [WILLIAM GARNETT]

Pine Ridge, So. Dak.
December 15, 1923.

Mr. Doane Robinson,
Pierre, So. Dak.

Dear Sir: Please pardon my delay in answering your letter of December 5, 1923, but I have been absent from the Agency and could not attend to it before.

I interpreted for Red Cloud when he gave his family history for the Pine Ridge Agency, and he gave the name of his father as Red Cloud. This, I am absolutely positive, was not his father's name, but was the name of an older brother of Red Cloud, from whom he took the name. His father was named Lone Man or Only Man, and his mother was named Walks As She Thinks. They were both members of the Old Smoke band of the Oglala Sioux.

I am unable to say whether or not the story of Red Cloud by James H. Cook is authentic or not, but if you will send me a copy I will read it over and will return the copy and let you know how true it is.

Red Cloud spent considerable time at Mr. Cook's place, and they were quite friendly, and very likely Cook got his information from Red Cloud himself, and if he did, it is very likely to be a little overdrawn, for when an Indian, and especially an old one, and a chief, is telling about himself, he leaves out very little, and is apt to stretch a point occassionally.

Very truly yours, [WM. GARNETT]

---

April 4th, 1924

Edward S. Stewart.

Dear Sir: I was much pleased to receive your letter of the 29th, ult, and to know that some one was trying to help out my old interpreter, and on your suggestion I am taking the matter up with the Senators of California-Montana-North and South Dakota-Wyoming and Nebraska by personal letter with copy of inclosed statement.

Also with Garnetts relatives in Washington, to swing in Virginia influence.

I presume that you will care for Colorado.

Yours truly,      V. T. M'G.

---

HOTEL CLAREMONT
Berkeley, California

March 15th, 1926

Friend Garnett,   How are you getting along these days, I reached seventy seven years the fourteenth of last month.

I want to ask you some questions about the Custer fight on the Little Big Horn on June 25th. 1876, as I was surgeon of the 2d. Cavalry with Crook in the Rosebud fight on the 17th, of June.

One question is, on that Sunday forenoon on the Little Big Horn, did the Indians know that Custer was approaching, or were they taken by surprise when Renos battallion attacked the upper end of the village,

Did they have scouts out over the country watching Crooks movements, also the movements of Custer.

Gen. Terrys command reached the Little Big Horn on Tuesday morning and the Indians pulled out.

On the day of the Little Big Horn Battle did the Indians know that Terrys main command was camped on Powder River, and would soon be coming up.

Who commanded the Indians at the upper end of the village where Reno attacked, Crazy Horse – Gall – or Crow King.

About how far was the Rosebud battlefield from the Little Big Horn.

How many fighting men do you estimate the Indians had that day.

We were completely taken by surprise at ten o'clock that morning at the Rosebud, and although we had 1100 men we were very glad to see the Indians pull out after a four hour fight, and why did the Indians do it.

There are so many "sole survivors" that just saved their hair in the Little Big Horn battle, bobbing up now and telling all about it, that I am beginning to wonder whether I know anything about it, or was ever in that country.

I wish the old days were back.  Good luck to you.

Yours,      V. T. M'GILLYCUDDY

---

HOTEL CLAREMONT
Berkeley, California

April 15th, 1926

Friend Garnett,   Many thanks for information in your recent letter.

Can you tell me, was the hostile village on the Little Big Horn, where Custer attacked, in the same location as it was when they came down and attacked us on the Rosebud on June 17th.

Are Frank Gruard and Louis Bordeaux both dead.

Did Crazy Horse ever have his picture taken, they claim to have one of him now, but I hardly believe it, for I tried hard to have one taken of him in 1877.

Was not his father an Oglala, and his mother an Huncpapa.

At what agency was Crazy Horse located in 1875 and in the Spring of 1876, when the Indians were organizing the hostile camp.

What agency or band did Touch the Cloud belong to, he was the Indian who sat up with me in the Adjutants Office at Fort Robinson when I was caring for Crazy Horse the night he died. How do you spell his name.

What agency or band did Little Big Man belong to, and where was he located in the Winter of 1875-6.

I am running across chaps now who were on nursing bottles in those days, and who know more about the days of 1876 than I do.

Yours,      V. T. M'GILLYCUDDY

---

Pine Ridge, So. Dak.
April 21, 1926.

Dr. V. T. McGILLYCUDDY.
Hotel Clairmont, Berkley, Calif.

Dear Doctor:   I have your letter of April 15, 1926, and you are advised that the hostile village was not on the Little Big Horn when the Indians came over and attacked your outfit on the Rosebud. They were camped on Dead Man in the Lodge Creek, which is a little creek that runs into the Little Big Horn, and is about 25 miles from where you were on Rosebud. The mouth of Dead Man in the Lodge Creek is something like forty miles above the Custer Battle Field.

Frank Gruard and Louis Bordeaux are both dead, Frank having died about 18 years ago and Louis about five years ago.

Crazy Horse never had a picture taken that I know of, and if there was one taken, some one sneaked up and took it, for he never would consent to be photographed. He was very peculiar about this, and was a very modest man, considering his fighting ability, and bravery.

His father was an Oglala and his mother was a Mni-Ko-Wo-Ju.

Crazy Horse was never located at any agency, and was out in the hostile camp in 1875 and 1876, but he came to the Red Cloud Agency when he was killed, he belonging to the Oglala band.

Touch the Cloud was Chief of the Mni-Ko-Wo-Ju band, having succeeded his father, Lone Horn, though he was with the Oglalas and the Spotted Tail Indians, with his band, during a large part of 1875 and 1876. He helped bring Crazy Horse in to Fort Robinson, and that is how he came to be in the Adjutants Office with you. I think he was a relative of the mother of Crazy Horse, but I have been unable to find any one who knows for sure.

Little Big Man was an Oglala, and a great friend of Crazy Horse, and was in his band. You will remember Little Big Man was holding Crazy Horse when he was stabbed, trying to keep him from fighting. He was out with him all during 1875, 76 and 77.

I am like you, and am continually finding people who were not born when these events took place; who seem to know more about them than you and I do, who were actually there.

Very truly yours,        [WM. GARNETT]

---

HOTEL CLAREMONT
Berkeley, California

April 26th, 1926

Friend Garnett,    Many thanks for your letter of the 21st, and the information contained therein for it clears several matters of which I have been in doubt.

I am surprised at the names of several of the old timers still alive, particularly of He Dog.

I enclose that picture of Crazy Horse recently published, I made up my mind that it was a fake, he evidently posed.

Crazy Horse was a strange looking Indian, and I would have known him any where.

You can return the picture anytime.

Some of these days I intend to write up what I know about the killing of Crazy Horse, he was a good man, and I would trust him any where.

Gen. Jesse Lee who was Lieut Lee in those days died a few days ago in Washington, he was completely out of his head for past year.

Yours truly,      V. T. M'GILLYCUDDY

---

HOTEL CLAREMONT<br>
Berkeley, California

May 8th, 1926

Friend Garnett,   More questions about Crazy Horse.

When Crazy Horse came in with his people to Fort Robinson in the Spring of 1877, why did he do so, do you think that he intended to remain peaceable and become an agency Indian, or did he intend to go North again.

You know his wife was very sick with consumption, and the Sunday the hostiles came in, I was sent for to come to the camp and give her medicine which was the first time I met Crazy Horse, and thus we became good friends.

There is a report that the sickness of his wife caused him to 'surrender,' what do you think about it.

What band did his wife belong to, and did she die before he did.

There is also a report that he got stuck on Louis Richards daughter, and bought her, and that she lived in his lodge with him, is this true, and if so did they live together before or after his sick wife died.

You know that the morning at daylight when the three troops of cavalry went out to arrest Crazy Horse I was sent along as medical officer, when we arrived the village was scattered and gone, how do you suppose they knew that we were coming.

There was a report got around that Crazy Horse when arrested was to be rushed through to Sidney Nebraska, and sent away to prison, did you ever hear that report.

Do you think the report was true that Crazy Horse intended to skip out North again, at that time and go on the War Path.

Yours truly,      V. T. M'GILLYCUDDY

They are going to have the fiftieth year anniversary on the Little Big Horn on June 25th, of the Custer fight, and want me to come over.

I am not going, I would meet too many Ghosts of my old comrades who were in the campaign of 1876, and too many of the 'sole survivors' who were not there in 1876.

Yours truly,      [V.T.M.]

---

HOTEL CLAREMONT<br>Berkeley, California

May 10th, 1926

Friend Garnett,   I am troubling you with more questions.

Where did Crazy Horse get his name.

Was his fathers name Crazy Horse, and was he a chief.

Was not Crazy Horse rather queer in his head.

The night that he was dying in the adjutants office,

and his heart was giving out about ten o'clock, I started to give him a glass of brandy, but the old man objected, making signs that his sons "brain whirled."

You remember that in March 1876 Crazy Horse had his big camp on Powder River west of the Black Hills, it was very cold weather,

He was attacked by Gen. Reynolds and the 3d. Cavalry, and his camp and ponies captured.

He got back at Reynolds next day, stampeded and recovered his ponies.

About how many people were in the camp, were there women and children, were there many killed.

To what bands did the Indians belong.

How long had the camp been made up, and was Crazy Horse then preparing for the war path of the coming summer.

What agency if any did he then belong to.

Was Touch the Cloud out with the hostiles that summer.

Did not the Minne Conjus or Cheyenne River Sioux have special claim to the Black Hills as their country.

Was Little Big Man acting as a friend of Crazy Horse the day he was killed, or why was he with Capt. Kennington when they tried to put Crazy Horse in the guard house.

I was standing about thirty feet from Crazy Horse when he fell, and never quite understood the thing, you know I arranged with Gen Bradley to put him in the office.

Along through that Summer do you think that Crazy Horse was figuring on leaving the Red Cloud Agency with his people, and again going north to Montana.

I always liked Crazy Horse, he was a brave man, and a good man, but Lieut Clark distrusted him, and I think Gruard prejudiced Gen Crook and Clark against Crazy Horse, I never had any use for Gruard.

When Crazy Horse fell that day in September I saw Gruards head projected out from around the corner of the old commissary, and I tried to get him over to me to interpret, but he was too scared to come, in fact I did not feel very well myself, I finally got John Provost down from in front of my quarters.

At the Little Big Horn fight, at which end of the camp was Crazy Horses people, or in other words who did Reno run up against, Gall and Crow King, or Crazy Horse.

Yours,        V. T. M'G.

---

HOTEL CLAREMONT
Berkeley, California
October 3d, 1926

Friend Garnett,   Many thanks for your letters giving me information about the old days, and the people we used to know.

Frank Goings called at the hotel a few days ago, and my wife and self had a very pleasant visit with him for about two hours.

He is traveling with Sells and Flotows Circus, he appears to have turned out a very good man.

We talked over the old lively days, and checked up the dead, and there are certainly many of them gone, it makes me feel old.

I often feel like making a visit to the old agency, and running over the old ground, but I guess that I would regret it, every thing changed, the old time ones, whites and Indians gone, I wish that the old days could come back.

## The Killing of Chief Crazy Horse

As I look back the Oglalas were very good people and meant well, I was young in those days, and I had to come down pretty hard on them at times, and some did not understand what I was trying to get at, but I meant it all for the best, old Red Cloud and I quarreled, but I expect that if I had been in his place I would have had less use for the agent than he had.

I saw the coming of the changes, and the crowding in of the white man, and it was my duty to prepare the younger Indians for the day coming when they would have to meet the white man at his own game, many of the Indians did not understand me, particularly the older ones, but the young men stood by me, and I never forget it.

You, Billy I shall always remember as the best inter-preter we ever had.

Goings tells me that Big Bat, is losing his eye sight, he was a good man, I shall always remember him at the Slim Buttes battle, remember me to him.

Yours truly,      V. T. M'GILLYCUDDY

---

HOTEL CLAREMONT
Berkeley, California

May 30th, 1927

Friend Garnett, Many thanks for the information given in your letter of the 24th, as it supports the infor-mation I obtained from officers and men of the 7th, Cavalry after Crooks and Terrys commands united in August 5th, 1876 at the mouth of the Powder River.

The burial party from Terrys command, who arrived on the field on Tuesday morning two days after the battle, told me that they found Custers body on a little gravel hummock, with the bodies of some of the officers and men, his body was on its back, stripped of everything but the stockings, one Winchester ball had entered the left temple, and another the right chest, it was not scalped or mutilated except for a knife slash in one thigh.

The most of the bodies of the men were badly mutilated, heads, legs, and arms cut off etc.

Major Reno informed that Custer wore a full buckskin outfit that day, and hair cut short, and there was nothing to mark him as an officer.

That man who broke away and was escaping, was I think, Dr. Lord, the Surgeon of the Batallion, as his body was never found, he was a friend of mine, some cowboys found the old skeleton of a man, about three miles East of the field, two or three years after, with scraps of uniform and army buttons. If he had kept on he would have run into Terry next day, on his march from Powder River.

Thanks for information on Pension Law, and I have sent for a copy, I have no pension, but would like one, they have a way of forgetting people.

I would like to visit the old crowd, and the agency again, and may some time, for I shall never forget my Oglalas, they were good people, I guess that I worried a good deal at times, but I was looking ahead, and doing my duty in trying to prepare them for the future that I knew was coming.

Yours,     V. T. M'GILLYCUDDY

---

Berkeley Cal., June 24th, 1927

Friend Garnett,   I inclose another Indian dream, about who killed Custer, please read and return.

There was sent me recently two reports regarding, who or what caused the death of Crazy Horse at Fort Robinson Sept, 6th. 1877.

## The Killing of Chief Crazy Horse

One made by Lieut. Lemly who was Officer of the Day, that day, and the other by Lieut. Jesse M. Lee who was Acting Agent at Spotted Tail, and who brought Crazy Horse back to Ft. Robinson.

Lieut. Lemly states that Crazy Horse was arrested because he and Louis Richards daughter had run away and lived together, and that Crazy Horse would not give her up.

I remember hearing something of this before, and is there anything to it, and was Crazy Horses first wife who came in with him in the Spring of 1877 alive at the time.

Lieut Lee states that the council between Gen. Crook and Crazy Horse which broke up in a row, about Sept, 1st 1877, in which it is claimed that Crazy Horse threatened to go North with his people on the war path, was held at the Spotted Tail Agency. My recollection is that it was held in Crazy Horses camp about five miles from Ft. Robinson., where was it held?

I was pretty well mixed up in that affair.

About Sept. 1st, Crook arrived at Ft. Robinson from Omaha, and along in the afternoon I was on horse back alone on my way to Crazy Horses camp. about half way there I saw the Generals four mule ambulance coming on the jump towards me from the camp, and the General halted me and ordered me back to the post for the reason that it would not be safe for me to go into the camp as there had been trouble in the council.

That evening about eight o'clock Louis Bordeaux came to my quarters and remarked, "Doctor, that damn Gruard raised hell in the council today, for I was there, and when Crook asked Crazy Horse to take his young men, and help the Great Father, by going North and helping to round up Nez Perces, Crazy Horse said, you sent for me, I came in for peace, I am tired of war, but now that the Great Father, would again put blood on our faces, and send us on the war path, we will go North and fight until there is not a Nez Perce left, Gruard interpreted it, we will go North and fight until there is not a white man left." Bordeaux also stated that it was a put up job by Gruard, as he was afraid of Crazy Horse and wanted to get rid of him.

I saw the General after Bordeaux left, but Gen. Crook said, there was no mistake, Crazy Horse is figuring on going North to join Sitting Bull.

The next morning Crook struck out for Ft. Laramie by ambulance in a hurry.

The following day a courier arrived from Ft. Laramie with orders to arrest Crazy Horse and put him in the guard house, and I received orders to report next morning before daylight as medical officer to accompany the expedition to make the arrest.

When we arrived at the site of the village at daylight, there was not a lodge or Indian to be seen, they had scattered and gone.

That evening a courier came through from Maj. Burke commanding at Camp Sheridan that Crazy Horse had arrived in Spotted Tails camp, and orders were sent back to Burke to arrest Crazy Horse and return him to Ft. Robinson.

Burke was not hunting for trouble, so the next morning when Crazy Horse came to the office with Spotted Tail he was informed that the Commanding Officer wanted him to come back to Fort Robinson for a council, he was not searched or told he was a prisoner, so he agreed to go back, and he and Lieut Lee acting agent left with the ambulance at 9 A.M. accompanied by Bordeaux and a party of mounted Indian Scouts, neither Lee or Bordeaux were informed that he was a prisoner.

In the meantime at Ft. Robinson I had been ordered to keep within the limits of the post, as in case of trouble with the Indians I would be wanted.

Well I sort of smelled it in the air that trouble was coming.

About half past four the ambulance rolled up to the adjutants office, and I struck across the parade ground to go down and see Crazy Horse, and about half way across the parade ground I met Lee and Bordeaux headed for Gen. Bradleys quarters, and they were excited, for it turned out that when they entered the adjutants office they found no one but the Officer of the Day, Capt. Kennington, who informed Lee that he had orders to receive Crazy Horse and put him in the guard house, at that Bordeaux whispered to Lee, "we better get out of here, if they try to put him in the guard house, there will be a fight and we will get killed for bringing him over here."

When I arrived in front of the adjutants office there were about half a dozen line officers standing around, and crowds of Indians gathering. Kennington came out with Crazy Horse who half nodded to me, they passed along and entered the guard house quietly, and I thought it all over, when suddenly there was a howl from Crazy Horse and he jumped out the door, striking with his long knife at Kennington. Kennington and Little Big Man who was standing near caught hold of him, but he slashed Little Big Man across one wrist and freed himself, but the double guard of twenty men closed in around him with fixed bayonets, officers, orderlies, and interpreters had all disappeared and I was left standing alone about twenty five feet away, then he lunged from side to side trying to break through, when suddenly one of the guard a private of the 14th, Infantry made a lunge, and Crazy Horse fell to the ground. By that time as the cow boys would say "Hell was popping" the Indians milling around and yelling at us, etc, I wedged my way in between the guard and found Crazy Horse on his back, grinding his teeth and frothing at the mouth, blood trickling from a bayonet wound above the hip, and the pulse weak and missing beats, and I saw that he was done for, so I worked my way out again and informed Kennington, who said, "Well I have orders to put him in the guard house, and if you will take one shoulder, I will take the other, the men will take his feet, and we will carry him in" so we tried it, when a big Northern Sioux gripped my shoulder and partly lifting me, began making motions to leave him alone, which we were forced to do.

Things came to a stand still, so I suggested to Kennington that I would go up and see the General and explain matters, and I did so, and his reply was, "Please give my compliments to the Officer of the Day, and he is to carry out his original orders, and put Crazy Horse in the Guard House," so back I went, and seeing Gruards face sticking out from around the corner of the commissary, I called him to come and interpret, but he disappeared, I then saw John Provost my interpreter up in front of my quarters and called him across the parade ground to interpret, I explained to American Horse who sat on his horse that Crazy Horse was badly hurt, that orders were that he be put into the guard house and I would care for him, etc, his reply was "Crazy Horse is a Chief and can not be put in the guard house."

## The Killing of Chief Crazy Horse

So I made another trip across the parade ground to see the General, I explained the condition, that he had eight hundred men under arms, had men enough to put Crazy Horse in the guard house, but I said "General it will mean the death of a good many men and Indians before you succeed, for the Indians are ugly," the old chap hated to give in, but finally agreed to my proposition to put him in the Adjutants Office where I could care for him.

I gave him hypodermics of morphine which eased his pain, he died about midnight, no one came to the adjutants office that night and it was dismal and lonesome, the only ones present were Capt. Kennington Officer of the Day, Lieut Lemley Officer of the Guard, Old Crazy Horse, the interpreter, Touch the Cloud, and myself.

Old Crazy Horse wailed and said, "We are Northern Sioux, we do not want to live on the white mans beef, we prefer to hunt our buffalo, but the Grey Fox kept sending out to us, Come in, Come in, we came in, they have killed my boy, Red Cloud, Gruard, and the agency Indians are jealous of us."

If Crazy Horse had not been killed he would have been taken that night, to the rail road, and Ft. Marion Florida.

When I went to my quarters that night, Touch the Cloud went with me and slept on the floor until morning, things looked scary.

I wonder who was responsible for his death.

Yours truly,      V. T. M'GILLYCUDDY

HOTEL CLAREMONT
Berkeley, California

Sept. 30th, 1927

Friend Garnett,   Many thanks for your letter of the 3d.

I would like to have got around to Pine Ridge, but the same as you I am getting old and it is a long ride, and it would have been lonesome, for nearly all of my old acquaintances are gone, and all that remains is their ghosts that come back to me in my dreams.

I am over seventy eight, but have not spent a day in bed for sickness in over sixty four years, I have a bullet in my skull and several broken bones, but they are accidents.

I am sorry I missed seeing Dr. Carver, I was expecting him here when I received your letter.

I inclose a newspaper clipping, about the Indian who killed Custer, it certainly took a good many to do it, I suppose another one will come to life after a while, like the old scout who was the sole survivor.

I noticed in a newspaper yesterday, that Dr. Royer who lives in Southern California is in trouble for using too much morphine.

I received a letter from Hank Simmons widow the other day, she lives in Southern California.

You can return the newspaper clipping some time when you are writing.

I would like to get back and see you, and the remainder of the old crowd, and may be I will, for I am getting pretty lonesome, and I liked my Indian life, and my Indian friends.

I suppose I made some mistakes as agent, for I was young, but I did what I at the time thought was best.

If I had been Red Cloud, raised as he was, I expect that I would have tried to raise the devil with the agent.

Yours,         V. T. M'GILLYCUDDY

---

HOTEL CLAREMONT
Berkeley, California

October 4th, 1927

Friend Garnett,   The Photographic Division of the War Department in Washington, has just issued the inclosed photograph claiming that it is a picture of Crazy Horse.

It certainly does not look like him as I remember him.

I never knew of his having a photograph taken.

What do you think about it, and who is this Indian, and later on return it to me.

Yours truly,         V. T. M'GILLYCUDDY

---

HOTEL CLAREMONT
Berkeley, California

October 8th, 1927

Friend Garnett,   You will notice by the inclosed newspaper clipping that the old agent Dr. Royer has been getting into trouble, taking too much morphine or opium.

People East are now asking me questions about the Black Hills.

A newspaper editor in New York City wishes to know who owned the Hills before the Sioux.

Was it not the Crows, and if so how long ago, and how far did the Crow country extend North and South, and East and West.

How long ago did the Crows live in the Hills, and did they have permanent homes or camps there, or merely go in for lodge poles, fruit, and hunting.

When the Crows held the Hills, how far East did the Sioux range.

We have a peak on the West side of the Hills that I ran onto in my survey in 1875, called Inyan Kara.

Is there any such word in the Sioux as Kara.

The peak has a high rock center, and should not the name be, Inyan Kaga Paha, the rock made hill.

Yours truly,    V. T. M'GILLYCUDDY

---

HOTEL CLAREMONT<br>Berkeley, California

October 25th, 1927

Friend Garnett,   Another question.

Crazy Horse was in camp on "Dead Man in the Lodge Creek" which he started from when he swooped down upon us June 17th, 1876. at the Battle of the Rosebud, where he took Crook by Surprise and gave us such a shaking up.

Can you tell me just where Dead Man in the Lodge Creek is.

What direction was it from the Rosebud, and what does it empty into.

Have you any idea offhand, how many Indians were killed and wounded at the Rosebud, and how many at the Little Horn.

What do the Indians call the Custer Battlefield, The Little Horn, or the Little Big Horn.

After the Custer fight, the hostiles on Tuesday abandoned the field and struck North, now how long did Sitting Bull and Crazy Horse hang together, and how long was Sitting Bull in getting across the line, leaving Crazy Horse in Montana.

Yours truly,    V. T. M'GILLYCUDDY

# The Killing of Chief Crazy Horse

Pine Ridge, So. Dak.
December 14, 1927.

Dr. V. T. McGillycuddy.
Hotel Clairmont, Berkley, Calif.

Dear Dr. McGillycuddy: I have been up and down for the last three months, and feel pretty good some times and others I am no good for anything, but I will try and answer your several letters, taking them in the order I received them.

I am returning the newspaper clippings and the photograph of the Indian who is supposed to be Crazy Horse. As you know, Crazy Horse was an Indian just a little past 30 years old when he was killed, and this picture is of an old man. Crazy Horse never wore a War bonnett in his life and I am very sure he never had a photograph taken. If I am not mistaken, there was nothing in the picture line but tin types up to the time of his death, the photograph prints having been invented later. The photograph is of a Rosebud Indian named Goes to War, a brother of Hollow Horn Bear of Rosebud, Hollow Horn Bear having been quite a chief before he died.

Before the Sioux Indians owned the Black Hills they were in the country occupied by the Kiwah Indians.

The Crow Indians occupied a country roughly described as the western part of Nebraska, all of Wyoming, and southern Montana. Of course they hunted and fought over more territory than this, but that was their regular range.

The Crows never owned the Black Hills, but they used to sneak in there and hunt, pick fruit and get lodge poles. They never had permanent homes there and were always run out by the Sioux as soon as they found they were there.

The word Inyan Kara is not a Sioux word, though I am of the opinion that it originally was, and the spelling has been corrupted until it can not be recognized. Inyan is an Indian (Sioux) word, meaning rock or stone.

Crazy Horse was not camped on Dead Man in the Lodge Creek, which runs into Tongue River, but was camped on Move Creek, which runs into the Little Big Horn, before they attacked your outfit in the Rosebud fight. They went about 20 miles to make the attack, the camp moving at the same time, down the creek so the fighting men did not have to go back to the old camp after the fight.

Very truly yours,     [WM. GARNETT]

**LIEUTENANT WILLIAM PHILO CLARK AND THE
SIOUX, LITTLE HAWK**

Courtesy of The Smithsonian Institution, Bureau of American Ethnology.

Baptiste "Little Bat" Garnier

THE FAMILY OF BAPTISTE "LITTLE BAT" GARNIER

From the left: John Garnier, a son; a daughter; Little Bat; a daughter; Garnier's wife with younger children. Mounted men not identified.

Courtesy of Nebraska State Historical Society.

# Lieutenant William Philo Clark
## Second Cavalry

William Philo Clark was born in New York state in 1845, entered the Military Academy in 1864, and graduated June 15, 1868, as a Second Lieutenant, being assigned to the Second Cavalry, in which he served the remainder of his life, except for his many special assignments as aide-de-camp to Sheridan and Crook, his marvelous study of the Indian Sign Language, and his numerous other frontier duties.*

He was known to his fellow officers as "Philo," to the enlisted men as "Nobby" and to the Indians as "The Chief with the White Hat." He proved to be one of the ablest of the young officers coming along after the Civil War, commanded troops in the field, had an excellent record as a staff-officer and more than fulfilled the expectations of his superiors. He died suddenly in September 1884, while on special duty in Washington with General Sheridan, at the early age of 39.

He fully deserves an entire book to himself, but our connection with him in this study concerns his "cloak and dagger" work in the death of Crazy Horse. He was probably the best man in the army for this particular job, especially when working under Crook and Sheridan; he was able and ruthless, and had the reputation of feeling and thinking like the Indians themselves. Crook also had the reputation of thinking like an In-

---

* Clark's greatest fame would come in connection with the tremendous amount of work, study, and travel he did in writing *Indian Sign Language,* (Philadelphia, L. R. Hamersly & Co., 1885), published after his death.

137

dian. Lieutenant Clark had a job to do, and he did it to the complete satisfaction of Crook and Sheridan.

Here are Crook's own words, written shortly after Clark's completion of the Crazy Horse job: "Lieut. Clark served under me during the campaign against the Sioux, organizing & commanding the scouts during the latter part of that campaign, & subsequently, *virtually controlled the Indians at the Spotted Tail & Red Cloud agencies,* rendering valuable services to the government in that campaign. Lieut. Clark also rendered efficient services during the Sioux Campaign of 1876, where he showed himself to be a bright and intelligent officer."

Leut. Clark's service just before this Crazy Horse incident consisted of serving as aide-de-camp to Brigadier General Crook from August to November, 1876, during which he was on the Powder River Expedition and took a prominent part in the Battle of Slim Buttes September 9, 1876. A series of engagements with various bands of Indians left the Army in relatively good control, and in anticipation of the coming changes Clark was sent to Fort Robinson in January 1877. He served there until November of that year except for a few weeks in September and October while he escorted a delegation of chiefs to Washington for negotiations there. So Clark was at Fort Robinson in May when Crazy Horse and his warriors surrendered, watching all happenings and getting reports through his spies in all of the various bands, holding pow-wows with the chiefs and warriors, with all of his plottings and actions pointed toward the accomplishment of the purposes of the War Department as set forth in the orders of Crook and Sheridan.

During this spring of 1877 the Sioux were in a desperate situation. True, they had overwhelmed Custer and his men just a few short months ago but since then they had been subjected to unceasing pressure from the War Department, with comparatively few bands (the most prominent of which was that of Crazy Horse) still out on the warpath. In the camps and reservations there was crowding and frustration, while promises of food and help were not fulfilled. One of the most destructive influences was the great jealousy and poisonous envy the various chiefs had for one another, and especially toward Crazy Horse. When Crazy Horse did come in on May 7th there was even more friction and back-biting, and you may be sure that Clark did his share to keep it going and building up. A rumor here, an innu-endo there, one chief apparently being favored over another, all these things kept the Indians divided just at a time when even a united front would not have been too effective in dealing with the whites. The old prin-ciple of "Divide and Conquer" was again proved effective.

# Baptiste "Little Bat" Garnier

In the various campaigns of the Army against the Indians, one of the most important individuals was the scout or guide; often the success or failure of the operation depended upon him. Usually he was a man, often a half-breed, who was familiar with the language and customs of the Indian tribesmen and who also had an intimate knowledge of the terrain in which the fighting might take place. In the Southwest Al Sieber and Tom Horn were of the greatest value. In the Sioux wars further north several names come to mind, among them Charlie Reynolds, Baptiste Pourier (Big Bat), Frank Grouard, Baptiste Garnier (Little Bat), William Garnett, Mitch Bouyer, and friendly Indians.

Among them all, however, none ranked higher than Little Bat in the estimates of the army officers. Born in 1854 of a French father and a Sioux mother, he was orphaned at an early age, living with various families, among them that of John Hunton. He married the daughter of a Frenchman named Mousseau and had a family of one son, John, and six daughters. It was from one of these daughters, Ella Howard, that the Crazy Horse tintype presented herein was obtained.

Little Bat became a most expert cow hand. As a hunter his skill was marvelous, and as a trailer he was known far and wide. No Indian could equal his trailing. One strong feature stood out above all others – his wonderful "bump of locality." Land him blindfolded in a strange country, and he would go as straight to his camp, in daylight or darkness, as the eye of a compass turns to the north. He was quite powerful physically and a tremendous runner. Grouard says he could chase a herd of elk and eventually kill them all by running them down into shooting distance.

He was thoroughly honest. He could be trusted with any property, and his promises could always be relied on. What he pretended to know, he knew.

One of Little Bat's most intimate friends was Capt. James Cook, of Agate, Nebraska, who speaks of him as follows: "We were close friends from 1876 to the day of Bat's murder. He was well thought of by all the officers and men who were ever associated with him. He was good-natured and even-tempered at all times. He was considered by Gen. Crook as one of the best big-game hunters in the Rocky Mountains.

"During the years that Little Bat and I were such close friends, I never knew him to have a quarrel with anyone. He was murdered by a scoundrel named Jim Haguewood, in Crawford, Nebraska, near Ft. Robinson, in December 1900."

"Bat was a man of more than ordinary intelligence. Although he possessed no school training, he had certain remarkable qualities that made him distinctive. His honesty and fearlessness were never questioned. His skill as a hunter, and his knowledge of the language, customs and manners of the Sioux made his services to the government invaluable. . .

"He was not a 'long-haired man of the plains' who had more hair than brains. He was a most modest and unassuming character of the frontier. His home and family, and the simple life of the Western pioneer were what he most desired. . ."

The above estimates and opinions were given by two very reliable men who knew Little Bat over a long time – John Hunton from the time of Bat's early teens, and Capt. Cook from about the age of 22 until Bat's death.

# William Gentles

William Gentles, a private of the Fourteenth Infantry, is a man of whom very few students of the Sioux Wars have ever heard, a man who lived and died of no consequence whatsoever, except for a few seconds on the afternoon of September 5, 1877. He was the man who killed Chief Crazy Horse.

We find the first mention of him on April 2, 1856, in New York City, where he had just enlisted in the United States Army for a period of five years. He is described as a native of County Tyrone, Ireland, 5 feet 8½ inches tall, grey eyes, brown hair, ruddy complection, a laborer twenty-six years old. His first assignment was to the Tenth Infantry, Company K. He served out his enlistment period, being discharged at Fort Laramie in 1861, in the meantime seeing duty in the Mormon War under Colonel Albert Sidney Johnston. Later in 1861 he enlisted in the First Missouri Volunteer Engineers and served during the Civil War. After the War he enlisted in the Fourteenth Infantry, which during the summer of 1877 was on duty in northwest Nebraska in the Fort Robinson region.

During the afternoon of September 5, Gentles was on sentry duty at Post #1, near the guard-house. There was considerable unrest and excitement, the Indians were in a turmoil because of the operations against Crazy Horse, and the army officers were prepared for all eventualities.

When Crazy Horse had been brought in, it was finally decided to put him in the guard-house, when he refused a struggle ensued, during which Gentles bay-oneted Crazy Horse through the kidney region, causing wounds and internal bleeding from which the Chief died about midnight.

Indian sources of the time did not know the name of the sentry but describe him as a heavy-set man with a full beard of a reddish color. While Gentles is listed as having brown hair, Mari Sandoz suggested to me that the red color could have come from the alkali dust of the region; this dust would bleach and redden hair.

After the stabbing Gentles was hidden from the ex-cited, milling Indians, and late that night was sneaked out to Camp Sidney. Grouard, whose intentional mis-interpretation started the whole unfortunate affair, also hid and escaped.

Gentles did not long survive his victim, dying the following May 20, at Fort Douglas, the cause of his death being listed as asthma. He was 48.

I have been unable to uncover any photo of Gentles, either in a single or in a group. However, here is a specimen of his signature:

# Bibliography and Index

# Bibliography

Anderson, Harry H. "Indian Peace-Talkers and the Conclusion of the Sioux War of 1876." *Nebraska History,* vol. 44, no. 4, (Dec. 1963) pp. 233-54.

Bordeaux, William J. *Custer's Conqueror.* Sioux Falls: Smith and Co., Publ., n.d.

Bourke, John G. *On the Border with Crook.* New York: Scribner's & Sons, 1891.

Brown, Dee. *Bury My Heart at Wounded Knee.* New York: Holt, Rinehart, Winston, 1970.

Brininstool, E.A. "Chief Crazy Horse: His Career and Death," *Nebraska History Mag.,* vol. 12, (Jan.-Mar. 1929) pp. 1-78.

Brininstool, E.A. *Crazy Horse, The Invincible Ogalalla Sioux Chief: The "Inside Stories," by Actual Observers, Of a Most Treacherous Deed Against a Great Indian Chief.* Los Angeles: Wetzel Publ. Co., 1949.

Byrne, P.E. *Soldiers of the Plains.* New York: Minton, Balch & Co., 1926.

DeBarthe, Joe. *Life and Adventures of Frank Grouard.* Edited with an Introduction by Edgar I. Stewart. Norman: Univ. of Okla. Press, 1958.

DeLand, Charles E. "The Sioux Wars (Part II)," *South Dakota Historical Collections.* Vol. XVII (1934), Pierre, S.D., pp. 177-551.

Hyde, George E. *Red Cloud's Folk.* Norman: Univ. of Okla. Press, 1937.

Hyde, George E. *Spotted Tail's Folk.* Norman: Univ. of Okla. Press, 1961.

Lemly, H.R. "The Passing of Crazy Horse," *Military Service Institution Journal,* vol. 54 (1914) pp. 317-40.

McGillycuddy, Julia B. *McGillycuddy, Agent: A Biography of Dr. Valentine T. McGillycuddy.* Stanford, Calif: Stanford Univ. Press, 1941.

## The Killing of Chief Crazy Horse

Neihardt, John G. *Black Elk Speaks: Being the Life Story of a Holy Man of the Oglala Sioux.* New York: Wm. Morrow, 1932.

Olson, James C. *Red Cloud and the Sioux Problem.* Lincoln: Univ. of Neb. Press, 1965.

Robinson, Doane. *A History of the Dakota or Sioux Indians.* Minneapolis, Minn: Ross & Haines, Inc., 1956.

Sandoz, Mari. *Crazy Horse, Strange Man of the Oglalas.* New York: Alfred A. Knopf, 1942.

Vestal, Stanley. *Warpath and Council Fire.* New York: Random House, 1948.

Schmitt, Martin F., ed. *General George Crook, His Autobiography.* Norman: Univ. of Okla. Press, 1946.

Standing Bear, Luther. *My People the Sioux.* Edited by E. A. Brininstool. Boston: Houghton Mifflin, 1928.

# Index

# The Killing of Chief Crazy Horse